# Dance Improvisations

# DANCE

# Improvisations

Joyce Morgenroth

UNIVERSITY OF PITTSBURGH PRESS

Published by the University of Pittsburgh Press, Pittsburgh, Pa. 15261
Copyright © 1987, Joyce Morgenroth
All rights reserved
Manufactured in the United States of America
Printed on acid-free paper

10    9    8    7    6


**Library of Congress Cataloging-in-Publication Data**

Morgenroth, Joyce
    Dance improvisations.

    Bibliography: p.
    Includes index.
    1. Improvisation (Dancing)  I.  Title.
GV1781.2.M67    1987        793.3'2        86-19318
ISBN 0-8229-3550-3
ISBN 0-8229-5386-2 (pbk.)


A CIP catalogue record for this book is available from the British Library.
Eurospan, London


"Mock Orange" by Karen Brodine is reprinted by permission of the author.
Photographs are by Jon Crispin.

# Contents

# Preface

This collection of improvisational problems grew out of my teaching college courses in dance technique, composition, improvisation, and movement for actors, plus summer improvisation workshops. In these classes, I inevitably brought my own understanding and preferences to the work. These inclinations remain in this book, particularly the two goals I have always sought: invention and its taking shape through the use of structure. I have aimed, in addition, for this book to be thorough and to cover all areas that relate to dance and movement for the theater.

The presentation of the improvisational problems varies in format. Some problems are presented as a single procedure, some as a series of procedures building to a final development. Occasionally I have included variations. I hope that readers will find their own variations as well. I have included observations after many of the problems, sometimes to clarify goals, sometimes to prepare the leader for difficulties the group might encounter, sometimes to generate thought about the work just done.

The ideas presented here offer a starting point and a way to proceed. The rest is up to the dancers.

One final note. To avoid the awkwardness of "he or she," I have used he and she alternately as subject.

# Acknowledgments

My thanks go to Peggy Lawler, my colleague at Cornell University, whose inspiration over the last twenty years has been immeasurable, from the first dance composition class I took with her to her most recent comments on my writing, and whose improvisational ideas appear throughout this book; to Jane Mushabac, who read my manuscript at every stage (on demand), and never failed to have incisive suggestions for improvement; to Fred Lee, who asked discomforting questions that helped me give shape to the manuscript; and to Moss Sweedler, whose seemingly casual suggestion was the impetus for my writing this book. I also thank Wendy Rogers of the University of California at Berkeley, Jessica Fogel of the University of Michigan, and Karen Bell of the Ohio State University for trying out these improvisations in courses they teach and for their encouragement. An improvisation workshop led by Richard Bull, Peentz Dubble, and Cynthia Novack is the source of several of the improvisations that are now among my favorites. Jon Crispin took the excellent photographs of the dancers: Pedro Alejandro, Karen Bell, Philip Bennett, Jessica Fogel, Nancy Gaspar, Janice Kovar, Holly Lau, Peggy Lawler, Fred Lee, and Sue Penney. I am grateful for other help I got along the way from Kevin O'Neill, Arnold Aronson, Les Thimmig, David Borden, Arthur Morgenroth, and my editor, Catherine Marshall. And since dance improvisation depends finally on the people who are doing it, I heartily thank my students and fellow dancers.

# Recent History

Improvisation has reemerged in the last twenty-five years as a powerful presence in dance and theater. The Judson Dance Theater and other groups whose work was based on improvisation, like the Second City, the Living Theatre, and the Open Theater, were a rousing and often disconcerting revitalization of the art of performance.

Western theater has a long history of improvisation. The troubadours of the Middle Ages and the Commedia dell'Arte of the Renaissance were important and accepted modes of theatrical performance in their times. In contrast, the recent upsurge of improvisation, flowering in the rebellious sixties, did not fall comfortably into our theatrical tradition. It broke rules of presentational decorum, violated traditional forms, and usurped the role of the choreographer and playwright. Few assumptions were safe. The artistic and political status quo were being assaulted.

Modern dance, in the first half of the twentieth century, had made a determined break from traditional ballet. By the 1950s, however, it appeared to have settled into its own traditions. By that time, on the West Coast, Jenny Hunter and Ann Halprin were working with movement improvisation, and in the East, Merce Cunningham, in close association with John Cage, was introducing radical innovations to choreography which were, in effect, a democratization of dance. Cunningham did away with the star system; all dancers were treated as equals on stage. The space itself was decentralized, giving equal value to all areas and requiring the audience to choose for themselves where to focus. In a major departure from the completely set choreography of traditional modern dance, the dancers were given certain choices to make in performance. Where formerly the primary value had been the artistic control by the choreographer, there was now an excitement about seeing choices being made at the moment. The intelligence of both dancers and audience was being engaged in a more active way.

In the early sixties the composer Robert Dunn taught a series of courses in dance composition at the Cunningham Studio. He had studied music composition with John Cage and used Cage's nonjudgmental approach to teaching. Dunn did not ask the students to consider whether a work was good or not, only what structure, form, method, and materials it used. As can be imagined, a new sort of work was appearing. An energetic, antitraditional spirit of exploration prevailed. Everything was open to question: the idea of phrasing, choreographic climaxes, technical proficiency, logical or dramatic continuity, the separation between performers and audience, and theatrical transformation. In July 1962, the class presented a public performance at the Judson Memorial Church on New York's Washington Square. This was the historic beginning of a new era in dance that was to include nontraditional methods of choreography and an increasing use of improvisation both in choreographing and performance.

Several of the original Judson dancers, who were to become the vanguard of postmodern dance, went on to work with Yvonne Rainer in her Continuous Project–Altered Daily. In 1970 Rainer decided to divest herself of authority over her dancers. She urged the group to work improvisationally without a leader. This move took Cunningham's democratization a step farther by eliminating the choreographer. Out of this change came the Grand Union. From 1970 to 1976 this group (ultimately comprised of Trisha Brown, Barbara Dilley, Douglas Dunn, David Gordon, Nancy Lewis, and Steve Paxton) performed what Sally Banes has called an extraordinary and entertaining combination of "dance, theatre, and theatrics, in an ongoing investigation into the nature of dance and performance" (*Terpsichore in Sneakers*, p. 203). The Grand Union was an arena in which these dancers discovered and elaborated their own methods and styles.

The choreographic work that has since been produced by the various members of the Grand Union carries signs of its improvisational precursor. It is highly individual and tends to expose the process of making dances, even in set pieces. Trisha Brown has included extemporaneous spoken instructions to the dancers that structure the piece in performance; Douglas Dunn has elicited audience participation, both physical and verbal; David Gordon has mystified audiences by confounding what is spontaneous and what is set; and Steve Paxton has been one of the main forces in the development of Contact Improvisation.

Also inherent in this change was the recognition of the vitality and uniqueness of live performance. In all of this work there is more interest in the process than in the product. Unlike works of art that can be bought and sold, or "canned" performances on film and television, live performance is a phenomenon of the moment: passing and ephemeral. There is nothing concrete to hold on to when the performance is over, especially with dance and unscripted theater events. The people making innovations in improvisational dance and theater valued this immediacy.

During the Judson period, the theater world was also undergoing a revolution. As with dance, there was a strong reaction against tradition, and an urge to redefine theater. This manifested itself in a break with linear narrative forms and the dependence on written scripts. This reaction also predicated a new involvement by the participants and audience, with particular implications in the political sphere.

In New York in the late fifties and early sixties, and in Europe after that, Julian Beck and Judith Malina's Living Theatre espoused an improvisational process of creating theater and interacting with the audience. Influenced by Antonin Artaud and John Cage, in 1960 the Living Theatre presented Jackson MacLow's *The Marrying Maiden*. The text was created by chance operations; in each performance, indeterminate elements generated unpredictable juxtapositions. Through their confrontation with the audience, use of real time presentations, and involvement with issues of immediate, public importance, the Living Theatre was moving away from the illusionistic actions of the stage and toward theater as a way to incite action in real life.

Coming out of the Living Theatre, Joseph Chaikin and Peter Feldman developed the Open Theater in the early sixties. They were committed to the process of collaboration with their actors. An important part of their exploration was based on the teachings of Nola Chilton and the theater improvisations of Viola Spolin. Through working improvisationally, the actors found images that were important to them individually and in common. Through this process, the performers carried some of the responsibility for the artistic conception. The audience was confronted with the presence of a live performer rather than the representation of a character.

In performance, the fourth wall was being transgressed physically, with actors invading the space of the audience and audience coming into the playing area. It was being transgressed philosophically as well. Theater was trying to change the lives of the people who did it and saw it. The innovative forms of theater were out to change not just people's perceptions, but the social structure as well. Theater was to be like life—not an imitation of the real thing, but an experience with the same immediacy.

To the new, radical theater, words appeared to be an intellectual trap. Movement, instead, was the way to get at the heart of feelings. From the "happenings" of the late fifties to the recent work of Jerzy Grotowski, there persists a belief in the connection between emotion and physical actions. Movement improvisation has been, in its various forms, a way to get at human impulses, which, in turn, have been at the heart of effective theater.

While improvisation was gaining public visibility in performance, people were discovering that if improvisation was compelling to see, it was even more compelling to do. Improvisation was appearing in classrooms and studios as well as at rehearsals and performances. Dance teachers introduced improvisation into their technique classes and dance composition classes. Viola Spolin's *Improvisation for the Theater* became a standard textbook for acting classes. Improvisational methods were incorporated into the process of creating plays and dances. Dance therapists used improvisation as a way to work with their clients. Improvisation is finally gaining widespread recognition in education, therapy, and performance.

As with every new effort, this book owes immeasurably to the work of those who have paved—or, in this case, tramped—the way, from Viola Spolin's beautifully elaborated problem-solving methods to the come-what-may performances of the Grand Union. It has aimed to leave room for individual inspiration while offering a coherent group process. The method presented in this book, structured dance improvisation, is a way of approaching dance simultaneously from two sides: conceptualization and action. While the formulation of each improvisational problem focuses the choices of the dancers toward a common structural goal, the dancers must respond physically at the instant to each other's movement. Structured group improvisation emphasizes the process of integration in three areas: the individual with the group; new skills with the skills that have already been practiced; and physical inventiveness with structural intuition.

Structured improvisation is a mixture of conscious choice and spontaneous reaction. It includes periods of sustained concentration and moments of unreproduceable magic. By responding to each other's imagination, intelligence, style, and energy, the dancers find themselves breaking through the patterns of thinking and moving that have limited them. Witness the spontaneous outburst of laughter and applause at the end of a successful improvisation.

# Practical Considerations for Leading an Improvisation Group

## ORGANIZING AN IMPROVISATION GROUP

The leader of an improvisation group may be a teacher, a choreographer, a director, a therapist, or one of the dancers in the group. Although leaders must organize sessions to suit their own circumstances, here is a quick survey of considerations that may be useful.

Dance improvisation does not require prior skill. However, a group that includes both very experienced dancers and inexperienced dancers can be frustrating. If this situation arises, the dancers can group themselves according to level some of the time. If appropriate, the improvisations can be adapted so that the beginners have simpler versions to work with. Then the more experienced dancers can work together for a while, for the satisfaction of working at their capacity. In some circumstances, a mixed group can provide the stimulus of different perspectives and thus benefit everyone.

Many of the improvisations can be adapted to groups as small as three and as large as thirty, though I have found a group of ten to twelve dancers optimal. Twelve dancers can divide easily into smaller groups, either working simultaneously or with some dancers watching while the others are moving. Or, for simply structured improvisations, twelve can work as a whole.

The best place to work is a clean, large dance studio with a suspended wooden floor. The group could also use a gym, a stage, a large room, or the outdoors.

The group might meet as infrequently as twice a week for one or two hours; or it might meet five times a week for four hours. One meeting a week is minimal if any group cohesion is to develop. The more regular the attendance, of course, the better the work progresses for everyone.

In most cases the leader of the group is responsible for determining the goal of the sessions, both overall and for each meeting—whether it is to introduce a creative perspective into a dance technique class, develop a dramatic scene, present methods of choreography in a dance composition class, or provide movement and character exploration for actors. In each context the leader can determine how great a challenge to present to the group, how much to emphasize gaining skill in movement, composition, and performance, and how much to emphasize the process of group improvisation as an end in itself.

# PLANNING A SESSION

The problems in this book are arranged topically for easy reference and are not necessarily in the order in which they are to be done. In general, limiting a session to one or two topics helps the group to develop and refine a given skill. Each topic includes some simple and some complex problems. "Simple" may mean solo or duet work or limiting choices for the group. The more complex group problems integrate composition with invention and allow more freedom of choice for the dancers. In any given session, working on a few simple problems can prepare the group for focused and exciting results from the more complex problems in the same area. The List of Improvisations at the end of this book indicates which improvisations may be appropriate for groups of various levels and sizes.

Since physical involvement as well as mental awareness is central to improvisation, the topics that include a good balance of movement and thinking can stand alone as a session. Some topics in the chapters on Space and Time that are more concerned with structure and practicing skills than with evoking movement exploration may be complemented by some more physically active problems from the chapter on Movement Invention. Then the session can end with a problem adapted to integrate both topics.

In choosing the sequence of problems for a session, the leader should keep in mind that the work done early in a session tends to affect what happens later. If the dancers do a problem that heightens spatial awareness, the awareness should help them through the whole session, even if the subsequent problems are not focused on space. More problematically, if they begin with slow movement, it may take a reminder to get them to move quickly and fully later.

Should music accompany improvisation? Music can establish an atmosphere and sustain the energy and concentration of the group. It also can set a pulse and act as the basis for rhythmic work or define the duration of an improvisation. It can unify the efforts of the dancers by influencing the style, speed, and energy of their movement. The danger is that the unifying effect of the music can substitute for attention to the other dancers. A good solution is to work with a live accompanist who can also react to the dancers, as well as having the dancers react to the music. Even with recorded music, though, the dancers can learn to react consciously to what they hear, just as they do to what they see. On the other hand, a concentrated silence can be the strongest accompaniment of all.

# RUNNING A SESSION

Every meeting should start with a warmup. The warmup should be within the leader's area of expertise and need not be technical. A technical warmup has the advantage of being thorough and improving the movement skills of the dancers; but it may also interfere with the exploratory process by offering a set movement vocabulary. For a nontechnical warmup that orients the dancers to the process of improvisation, see the problem Action Word Warmup in the beginning of the chapter on Preliminaries.

Once a general progression of problems is chosen for a session, it is important to be flexible in following this plan. The leader will need to be as responsive to the dancers as the dancers need be to each other. The leader will have to decide when to interrupt a problem, when to repeat a problem, whether to set a time limit or allow the problem to evolve without limits, and help guide the group toward a successful grasp of the work. The purpose of such choices is to help the dancers understand the focus of the problem so they will be able to work together effectively and with a sense of satisfaction.

The leader can help with beginnings and endings. One of the most avoidable faults of group improvisation is a chaotic beginning. In general, improvisations should start with only one person moving, so that each person who joins the improvisation does so knowing what is already happening. An improvisation can be started by someone who has the impulse to begin, or the leader may ask someone to start. Sometimes it helps to choose a dancer who will be capable of presenting effective material; sometimes the leader may encourage someone who would not otherwise take this initiative.

There are different ways to end an improvisation, but in all cases the dancers should get into the habit of ending with clarity, and holding their ending for an instant before disbanding. Before an improvisation begins, the leader may advise the dancers of an approximate length (e.g., one minute, half an hour). Then the leader may either call an ending, cue the dancers to find an ending, or let them find an ending when they feel the moment is right. Not every ending need be in stillness, and certainly not in the huddle favored by beginners. The dancers can imagine that the lights are dimming and continue to move through the fade-out. Or they can exit.

Discussion at the end of a problem or sequence of problems can help the dancers recall and assess the choices that they made, discover other possibilities that they might have tried, and understand consciously some of what they may have done by instinct. The discussions should not aim to decide what went right and what went wrong, but to understand the consequences of the choices that were made. If the group repeats the problem after their discussion, they can see how it is affected by their added awareness.

Not every improvisation is an immediate success. The leader will often have to troubleshoot, finding ways to rework problems. If a problem is boring to the dancers or to their audience (usually to both if to either), the dancers may have been missing the point. Making the focus clear to them may lead to more success. Simply persevering may also get them beyond their block. If a problem gets off to a bad start, with movement that doesn't work well within the structure, the dancers can start again with new material.

If too much is going on at one time, the difficulty may come from having too many people rushing in before they see what the others are doing. In general, a rule of thumb for most improvisations is to allow no more than two different events to occur at a time. The nature of an "event" depends on the topic being explored. It could be, for example, a grouping of dancers or a movement motif.

Sometimes dancers change what they are doing too often, not allowing others to see, understand, and find a response. It helps the improvisational process, which is often evolutionary rather than revolutionary, if the dancers tend toward being long-winded. This may occasionally feel slow, but it will often lead to a coherence that will have exciting results.

When a dancer breaks a rule of the improvisation it may be a means to avoid the crux of the problem. Sometimes it is a stroke of genius. The dancers should learn to know the difference. They should not get into the habit of evasion, for the intoxication of improvisation comes when the dancers' concentration is so engaged that responses are automatic. Then the structure is clear, the imagination is alert, and all the prior training has become instinct.

# Dance Improvisations

# I Preliminaries

Improvisation teaches skills; but it requires skill as well. Dancers must become accustomed to the process of improvisation and to its concentration and focus. They must be able to see and respond. These skills are practiced in the sections on Mirroring and Unison. Once these elements are in place, the dancers can begin to learn new skills and integrate them into their continuing work in dance.

When working with a group, individual invention is not as important as the ability to put one's invention to work in conjunction with others. This begins with an interest in working together and a feeling of trust for the other members of the group. The sections on Active and Passive roles and Weight Dependency help develop this foundation.

The daily preliminary to all movement is the warmup. This serves to prepare the dancers physically to move freely and safely. The Action Word Warmup that follows also puts the dancers in an improvisational frame of mind by eliciting memory, imagination, and the ability to imitate.

## ACTION WORD WARMUP

**Procedure** The leader names a type of movement. Some possibilities are: swing, stretch, twist, walk, run, bounce, fall and rise, shake. The group finds movement within the given category in these three ways: by spontaneous physical exploration; by drawing from past experience—movement learned in technique classes, learned in dances, seen in performance, or in life situations; and by imitating and varying what they see the other dancers doing. The dancers should keep moving continuously.

After a few minutes of exploring one movement category, the leader names another category. Alternatively, dancers may call out instructions, according to what they feel they need to warm up their bodies.

**Observations** If this is used as a warmup it is best to begin with easy movements like swings and walks, then runs and stretches, before doing any sudden movements or jumps.

With some prompting by the leader this activity can also help warm up the dancers' minds. The dancers can distinguish between reproducing familiar material, discovering new material, moving like someone else, and creating spontaneous variations. They can also pay attention to transitions between their own exploration and their imitation of others.

Because this exercise is simple, the leader can prompt the dancers to consider certain areas of their movement or performance that may need more attention, such as movement quality, use of focus, use of all parts of the body, and so forth.

### BODY PARTS WARMUP

Procedure    The dancers stand in a circle. One dancer names a part of the body. All the dancers move that part gently, then move it more fully. At any time another dancer may call out another part of the body. The dancers then move the new part named. The group should go through the whole body this way. The dancers can repeat the process doing movements that are initiated by the body part mentioned but involve the entire body.

### LOCOMOTOR WARMUP

Procedure    Everyone lines up in single file behind one dancer. This dancer travels through the space, moving in ways that begin to mobilize various parts of the body. At any time another dancer can step to the head of the line and take over the leadership, initiating a new kind of locomotor movement. The movement should become gradually fuller and more vigorous.

The dancers should be careful not to do too much too soon. Any dancer who feels unprepared to do the movement the group is doing can step to the head of the line and initiate a different movement, or can do some variant that feels more appropriate to her body.

During this warmup the dancers should travel through the entire space rather than remaining in the center.

## MIRRORING

Mirroring is the most basic of improvisations. Even in its simplest form, where two dancers face each other and move as perfect reflections of each other, mirroring elicits skills essential to all group improvisation. The ability to perceive and reproduce movement is developed through imitating precisely; the ability to respond without delay comes from the necessity of remaining synchronized with one's partner; the ability to sustain concentration is encouraged by focusing very specifically on one other dancer; and the discovery of new movement comes through watching and reacting to another. Since every detail must be reproduced, the dancers also get a kinesthetic sense of moving like someone else. And finally, these skills in watching and reacting are a preface to group improvisation, in which dancers, at best, see and consider everything that is going on at any time, no matter how large the group.

The processes of leading, following, and interacting are inherent to all improvisation. The mirroring problems given here present opportunities to try out all of these roles and then to extend them. Once the dancers have some ability to mirror one another they can begin to play against their partners' movement, through variations. They also get a chance to react to more than one dancer at a time through group mirroring.

These problems are central to the improvisational process and can be repeated often. They could even be used to start each session, serving as a mental and physical warmup for the improvisations that are to follow.

## MIRRORING

**Procedure**  Dancers pair off, facing each other in their pairs. One is the leader, the other the follower. As the leader moves, the follower mirrors the movement as exactly as possible. The goal is to achieve movement so nearly in unison that an observer could not tell who is leading and who is following. This is as much the responsibility of the leader, whose attention should be on moving clearly and keeping the follower with her, as of the follower, whose focused attention can lead him to feel the connection of his movement with that of the leader.

After a couple of minutes, the dancers reverse roles and repeat.

**Variation**  The leadership passes back and forth between the two dancers. Exchanges may occur in quick succession, so that even the dancers may not be able to identify when the changes occur. The leadership may also remain for a period with one of the dancers. Neither dancer should specifically choose to hold on to the leadership or to avoid it.

**Observations**   To make exact mirroring possible, the leaders have to move fairly slowly and avoid sudden movements. They also have to look at their partners, so that the partners, as the mirror images, can look at the leaders.

Dancers needn't stay in one place. They can travel along their mirror or move toward and away from the mirror. They should not, however, move through the mirror. They should know clearly where the mirror is located.

Mirroring exercises serve several basic purposes. They require that dancers look at each other; they ask dancers to observe and reproduce movement carefully. The exchange of leadership promotes a flexibility in initiating and following movement, a skill which is central to group improvisation.

## MIRRORING WITH SUCCESSION

**Procedure**   Dancers pair off. One dancer in each pair is the leader.

In each pair the leader moves and the partner mirrors his movement. Sometimes the leader moves so that the partner can mirror exactly. At other times he will move quickly or with accents. The follower should not let this disconcert her, but should mirror in succession, creating a rhythmic variation with total confidence.

Dancers reverse roles and repeat.

## MIRRORING WITH MOVEMENT VARIATIONS

**Procedure**   The dancers pair off. One dancer in each pair is the leader.

The leader does some movement that is easy to mirror and some movement that is hard to mirror. When the movement is too fast or complicated to mirror accurately, the follower can do it in succession, or abbreviate the movement, or do a variation. Whatever she chooses, she should maintain the fullness and continuity of her performance throughout.

The leader may also provide moments of stillness or do repetitive movement, to allow his partner to develop variations more fully.

Dancers reverse roles and repeat.

**Variation**   The dancers divide into groups of three or four. In each group one dancer is the leader while the others mirror with movement variations. The followers may find ways to respond to each other's variations as well.

**Observation**    Paying attention to the reactions of his followers should help the leader decide when to repeat his movements and when to introduce new motifs.

### GROUP MIRROR

**Preparation**    A line running down the center of the space is designated as the mirror. It may help to chalk or tape the line for visibility.

**Procedure**    Half the dancers are the audience. The dancers in the space pair off. One dancer in each pair is the leader. All the leaders begin on the same side of the mirror, with their partners opposite them.

   The leaders move and their partners mirror as precisely as they can. The leaders should interact with each other, paying particular attention to the spatial arrangement of the group as a whole.

   A leader may exchange roles with her partner whenever she chooses by approaching the mirror, touching the palms of her hands to her partner's, and exchanging places through the mirror. In this way, leaders are always on one side of the mirror.

**Observations**    This problem works best when it allows a greater range of movement than was possible in Mirroring. Followers should do their best.

   This exercise may be limited to focus on a particular skill. For example, the dancers may be asked to pay special attention to their floor pattern, levels, or rhythm.

## UNISON

There is a special pleasure in moving in unison with others, perhaps because it engenders a feeling of agreement and support—or anonymity.

   Unison, like mirroring, is an exercise in imitation. However, with its suggestion of mass movement, unison gives a more primitive and less personal effect than the more intimate mirroring. It allows the focus to be addressed outward. The movement is also free to roam the space, unlimited by the imaginary mirror. This means that the dancers get to explore their use of space in a context in which they need not also be concerned with complex movement choices. The simplicity of the unison group movement makes the use of the space clearly visible.

   Practice in keen observation and precise imitation is essential in learning movement, whether in dance class or rehearsal. It is also basic to all the work in group improvisation that is to follow, which depends on seeing what others are doing and reacting to it.

## NAME ACCUMULATION

**Preparation**  Each dancer makes up a short movement phrase to be accompanied by saying his or her name. The name may be pronounced along with the movement, before it, or after it. Dancers can play with rhythm and volume in saying their names. They shouldn't whisper them shyly.

**Procedure**  All the dancers stand in a circle. A dancer designated by the leader goes first. She performs her phrase accompanied by saying her name, say, Peggy. She repeats this once. Then the whole group repeats the movement and sound once in unison.

   The second dancer repeats Peggy's phrase, with sound, and adds his own movement and name, say, Moss. He repeats these two phrases. Then everyone repeats the sound and movement in unison. This process continues: Peggy, Moss, Philip, Holly . . .

   The leader can choose to interrupt the cycle and start again with the next person if the sequence is getting too long for the group to remember.

**Variations**  Using names helps a new group get acquainted. But the improvisation can also be done using any sound accompaniment, or in silence.

## GROUP UNISON

**Procedure**  The group begins in a cluster in the space, all facing in the same direction. The dancer who seems to be at the head of the group begins to move. The others move in unison with this dancer. As the facing of the movement (and therefore, the group) changes, so does the leadership. It is always the person who can't see any of the others who becomes the leader. In case two dancers standing next to each other aren't sure which one should lead, they should decide as quickly and simply as possible. In the case where a leader bends over and sends her focus behind her, whoever is visible at the opposite side of the group then becomes the leader. Dancers should aim to have smooth transitions from leader to leader, inter-

**Group Unison**

rupting the movement as little as possible. The group should always try to maintain unison.

The leaders should keep in mind that others are trying to follow them and should choose their movement accordingly. The movement needn't remain totally stationary, however. The group can move through the space and change levels. Other dancers may change places within the group during traveling movements, so that the leadership is not always passed on to the same people on the outer edges of the group.

**Variation**   Dancers divide into groups of three. Space permitting, all the trios may be in the space at the same time. Each trio arranges itself into a triangle, with all three dancers facing in the same direction. The dancer who has his back to the other two is the leader.

In this smaller format, the leaders can test the limits of the kind of movement possible for the others to follow. They may travel and use any range of dynamics. The followers imitate as best they can.

When the leader turns toward one of the other dancers he passes the leadership to that dancer. The dancers should eventually experiment with increasingly frequent exchanges of leadership.

### FOLLOWING TWO LEADERS

**Procedure**   Part of the group is audience. At least five dancers are in the space. Two dancers in the space are chosen to be leaders. The dancers distribute themselves so that each one can see at least one of the leaders.

The leaders move as they wish, keeping their backs to their followers. The followers may imitate either leader, from near or far. They may change from one to the other at their own discretion, maintaining their performance presence through the transitions.

**Observations**   The leaders have an important role, by determining not only the movement, but the relationships between the two groups. They may contrast level or speed, or keep one group stationary while the other travels, or establish a movement dialogue between the two groups. A leader may also be still for a period.

The followers determine the size and arrangement of the groupings. They also create moments of surprise as they change from following one leader to the other. These changes should occur rather frequently since they are a major part of the visual interest of this improvisation.

### THREE UNISON GROUPS WITHOUT LEADERS

**Procedure**   The dancers divide into three groups, not necessarily equal in size. Each group will move in unison, allowing the leadership to pass among the members of the group. In each group, the dancer who can't see any of the others is the leader. The three groups should interact with each other, relating design, dynamics, speed, and floor pattern.

Any dancer may change from one group to another at any time. At no time, however, should one group completely dissolve, though it may temporarily be reduced to a solo dancer. Dancers should find ways to maintain the continuity of their performance while changing groups.

A dancer must remain alert to the possibility that the person he is following might join another group at any moment. The dancer then has to choose whether to stay or change groups.

## ACTIVE AND PASSIVE

To improvise as a group, dancers must have respect and trust for each other's physical being and for the physical aspect of movement. They should not be afraid of physical contact with each other and should know how their contact can be safe and how it can communicate movement ideas.

The problems that follow deal with the roles of initiator and follower in a literal, physical way. This is "hands on" preparation for the exchange of initiative that occurs as dancers watch each other and react in movement to others' actions.

## MOVING WITH CLOSED EYES

**Procedure**  All the dancers close their eyes and turn around a few times to lose their orientation in the space. Then the dancers move through the space, exploring the floor, walls, furniture, fixtures. They can also explore slow-motion movement that they can safely do with their eyes closed.

If two dancers encounter each other, they may interact briefly, still with eyes closed.

**Observations**  Even in a familiar space, dancers may make discoveries about the size or shape of the space, or the location of objects within it.

This exercise also prepares them for the exercise in trust that follows.

## LEADING SOMEONE WITH CLOSED EYES

**Procedure**  The dancers pair off. One dancer in each pair closes her eyes. Her partner is responsible for leading her through the space. This should be done slowly at first. Where safety allows, the leader can lead his partner into more daring movement, such as running, waltzing, or sitting and rising.

Two leaders may exchange partners at any time. The followers should keep their eyes closed, so they don't know who is now leading them. Dancers should aim to move with ease and continuity even through changes of partners.

Dancers may exchange roles of leader and follower in two ways. The follower may open her eyes and meet the eyes of her leader, who then closes his eyes; or the leader may touch the forehead of his partner, who then opens her eyes, while the leader closes his eyes.

### ACTIVE/PASSIVE DUETS

**Procedures**   Dancers pair off. One dancer in each pair is active; the other is passive. After each of the first four procedures, dancers should reverse roles and repeat.

1. The active person is the sculptor, moving various parts of his partner's body into new positions. The passive person should allow the changes without resisting or adding any movement.

2. The active dancer gives movement impulses to his partner. This may be done, for example, by swinging his partner's hand, pushing his partner's hip with his own hip, or pushing his partner's shoulder with his hand. The partner should follow through only as much as the impulse genuinely requires, without either resisting or adding movement. After each movement the active dancer should allow his partner to be still before giving the next impulse.

3. As above, the active dancer gives movement impulses to his partner. This time the partner extends her response briefly, following through on the movement initiated by the impulse. Again, the active dancer allows his partner to stop before giving the next impulse.

4. The active dancer gives movement impulses to his partner, who now exaggerates her response, generating an extended phrase of movement out of the original response, or a large movement out of a small impulse.

5. The dancers play back and forth between the active and passive roles. In addition, each time a dancer receives an impulse from her partner she can choose, from the four ways already explored, how to react. This may be done in cooperation with her partner's apparent intention, or purposely in contrast to it.

Throughout the problem, the active dancer should not only initiate movement in his partner, but should find ways to dance through his own actions. He can sometimes be still as well, shaping his own body in relation to the shapes of his partner.

**Observations**   Dancers in the passive roles should be careful not to anticipate their partners, but should genuinely take their movement impulses from them. This way they can get a sense of their own body weight, inertia, and momentum.

Most dancers enjoy this problem because of the physical contact and the chance to push other people around.

**ACTIVE/PASSIVE GROUP**

**Procedure** This can be done by the whole group at once, or some of the group can watch.

Using the active/passive skills practiced in the last exercise, dancers may at will choose between the active and passive roles. They should consider the activity of the whole group in deciding when to change from one role to the other. An apparently passive dancer may surprise another dancer by suddenly becoming active.

Active dancers may relate to each other as well as to the passive dancers. Several active dancers may cooperate in moving one passive one. The dancers should explore the possibilities of group design among the static bodies.

**Observation** This problem keeps the fun of the preceding one and adds the interest of making compositional choices.

## WEIGHT DEPENDENCY

The amount of physical contact occurring between dancers has varied considerably over the years in both social and concert dance. Not so long ago most choreographers indicated contact with a gesture, but not with touching. By the seventies, however, with the advent of Contact Improvisation, based on the exchange of weight between dancers, people were lifting, leaning on, rolling over, pushing, and pulling one another in the name of movement and in the name of dance.

Weight Dependency offers dancers a use of their bodies and an interaction that provide, literally, a shared experience of movement.

**WEIGHT DEPENDENCY FOR TWO DANCERS**

**Procedures** Dancers pair off. They may wish to begin with partners of comparable size.

1. Partners face each other, toe to toe, holding both hands across (right hand to partner's left, left hand to partner's right). They lean away from each other, creating a balance of weight between them. Still leaning apart, the dancers both slowly sit, then slowly rise. The whole time their arms should remain straight, with shoulders (rather than hips) leaning away.

2. Holding hands in the same way, the two dancers lean away from

**Weight Dependency**

each other. One dancer sits while the other stays up, supporting her partner's weight. Keeping the pull between them, the dancers reverse roles, creating a see-saw effect. This can be repeated to a steady pulse.

3.  Partners face each other, toe to toe, holding right hands across. They lean away from each other, sit, and rise. Then they change to hold left hands across, sit, and rise. The dancers can establish a brisk, steady rhythm of sitting and rising with a change of hands at the top. The partners should keep the balance between them, neither one ever on balance individually. The moment of changing hands is a suspension, not a static point.

4.  Leaning back to back, dancers hook elbows and sit. They may have to walk their feet forward to be able to sit. They should move their feet as little as needed, so that they can take the weight on their feet as they rise together, still leaning back to back.

5.  Dancers can explore other positions of balance between them. They can try attaching different parts of the body, such as ankles, or arms

around each other's waist, and leaning away. They can also find a balance leaning against each other, trying various points of contact. Both dancers should keep off balance, so that if the connection between them were broken both would fall.

**Observation**  It is not necessary for partners to be of comparable size. Dancers should repeat some of the balances with bigger or smaller partners.

### FALLS AND CATCHES

**Procedure**  The dancers divide into groups of three. In each group, two of the dancers stand about four feet apart, facing each other. The third dancer stands between them, facing one of them. This dancer will alternate falling back, being caught by the person behind, and falling forward, being caught by the person in front. He should keep his body stiff, rather than let it go limp.

To catch someone, a dancer should begin fairly close, with her hands in front of her body, fingertips pointing up. She should catch the person's upper torso, taking one step back with bent knees, and then set the person upright.

Dancers exchange roles and repeat.

**Observation**  This exercise is done to sense and bear part of another's weight, and to develop physical trust among the dancers. Unless dancers are experienced in this sort of work, they should catch each other fairly close to the upright position.

### WEIGHT DEPENDENCY FOR A GROUP

**Procedures**  1. A group of dancers stands in a circle, holding neighbors' wrists. Everyone leans out from the circle, finding a balance within the group as a whole though no individual dancer is on balance.

2. In the same circle, dancers may sway and shift their weight. After a little while, an individual may leave his spot, move to a different point on the circle, and reattach himself in some way, not necessarily with his hands. He should again be off his balance. The group may rearrange itself into configurations other than a circle, always maintaining the weight dependency among the dancers, even through transitions, if possible.

3. Dancers may stand still or walk through the space. From time to time one dancer approaches another to do a series of balances. This should be done without words, merely by sensing the exchange between the two dancers. On occasion, a larger group may join together for a group balance.

### DUET SCENES

**Procedure**  All the dancers are in the space, paired off. Each pair explores ways to interact, drawing on the practice in active and passive exchanges and weight dependency.

After exploring some possibilities, the pairs should take five or ten minutes to prepare a sequence to show the others. This need not be set exactly, but should at least be conceived to have a beginning, middle, and end, whose exact content can be improvised in performance.

The dancers take turns showing their duets. If beginning dancers are shy at this point, several duets may be performed at once.

# II Space

Space is the visual medium in which we live. While we usually take space for granted, as a sort of passive arena for our perceptions, dance brings it into conscious play. The logistical question of visibility, the interest of group design, the impact of a mass of people, the changing configuration of a traveling group— all have a strong visual effect.

The chapter on Space is introduced early in the work because even the most rhythmically articulated, beautiful movement can lose its power if it is performed in a jumble of bodies. Learning to manipulate the use of space is probably the most important element of producing successful results in group improvisation.

## FLOOR PATTERNS

Covering space is exhilarating. Getting from one place to another conveys change, progress, expanse, and energy. The pattern made by the dancers as they travel through the space creates an immediate visual impact—often more powerful than the rhythms or the precise design of their movement.

Solo floor patterns created by moving through space may be planned or intuitive. When more than one person is in the space, the creation of coherent floor patterns within the group demands a cooperative effort. The purpose of the following improvisations is first to make the dancers aware of floor pattern as a means of structuring their movement and give them specific devices to work with. Then they are equipped to play with the endless possibilities.

### COVERING SPACE: QUICK SOLOS

**Procedure** The leader has a watch or clock with a second hand, for timing fifteen-second intervals.

The dancers are lined up in a corner of the space.

One dancer at a time covers as much floor space as possible in fifteen seconds.

**Observations**   After everyone has had a turn, the group may observe how they approached the problem. Was it at random or methodically? By a series of parallel lines? A spiral? A zigzag? A patchwork of smaller areas? A dancer might have gone down to the floor and rolled across the space, or extended her arms to suggest covering space.

Through this problem, the dancers can get a sense of the full extent of the floor space (the outer areas as well as the center), discover their own impulses for how to cover it, and see how others approach it.

## LOCOMOTION

**Procedure**   The leader calls out a mode of locomotion and the dancers move through the space accordingly. Examples include: walk (fast, slow, backward, sideways, pigeon-toed), limp, hop, run, roll, scurry, trip, slither, crawl, skip, leap, gallop, bound, lope, glide, chug.

Half the dancers may watch and call out new instructions.

**Variations**   1. Relay race. The dancers choose four modes of locomotion and set an order. They then divide into teams of four and arrange themselves in the space for a relay race. Each dancer in turn will travel his leg of the race in the prescribed mode of locomotion.

This encourages dancers to move fast and to move through the space. They may interpret the instruction imaginatively to help them do so. That is, they may find creative ways to cheat.

2. One at a time dancers travel across the space, trying not to repeat any movements on the way. For example, a dancer might run, leap, skip, lunge, roll, step-turn, chug, and slide.

**Observation**   Some beginning composition students tend to stand and think a lot and move very little. This problem can coax them to move through space.

## WALKING PATTERNS

**Procedures**   1. The whole group begins in the space. The leader calls out a series of instructions, to which the dancers immediately respond. The dancers should have about thirty seconds or one minute for each instruction:

a. Walk randomly around the space. See the other dancers.

    b. Interleave — Intersperse your walking with standing still.

    c. Walk only in straight lines parallel to the walls and make only right angle turns. Continue to intersperse your walking with stillness.

    d. Walk only in curved lines. Continue to intersperse your walking with stillness.

    e. Find an ending in stillness.

2. Once all the dancers are still, they repeat the instructions from memory. They should keep watching each other, so that once one dancer initiates a new phase, the others should soon join in.

**Observation**  Once the dancers have done this problem, they seem more aware of their facing in the space as well as their floor patterns.


### SOLO FLOOR PATTERNS

**Procedure**  The audience is located at one end of the space. To begin, one dancer takes a still position in the space.

This dancer improvises a solo with attention to the floor pattern, considering the use of curves, straight lines, small and large patterns, and her location in the space. Stillness is allowed. Each dancer in turn does a solo.

While keeping the floor pattern as the primary focus, the dancers should also be aware of other aspects of their movement: speed, rhythm, and dynamics, as well as the balance of movement and stillness.

Dancers should find their own endings. Like the beginnings, the endings should be strong and clear, with a definite final stillness.


### RIGHT, LEFT, ABOUT FACE

**Procedures**  1. Moving as a tight group, the dancers walk at a medium pace, parallel to one side of the room. At any moment any dancer may call out one of three directions: right, left, or about face. (They will discover the purpose of these commands as they approach walls or obstacles.) They may not stop or slow down.

2. In addition to the direction changes, the dancers may also call out fast, medium, or slow. There should be a definite difference between

these speeds. Transitions from one speed to another should be clear. As dancers change direction they should be careful not to let their speed drift to the medium range.

## TRAVELING AS A GROUP

**Procedure**    The dancers stand close together in the space.

Using a low, smooth run, the dancers move across the space. They keep as close as possible, while changing directions frequently. They will resemble a flock of birds or a school of fish. Anyone may initiate a change, with the others following as quickly as possible. Dancers should not be concerned with body design while they are traveling.

Dancers may stop occasionally. If one stops, they must all stop. A dancer may then choose to turn, change position within the group, or squat.

When one takes off, all must follow quickly.

**Observation**    Dancers must remain alert and be quick to respond to the group movement.

## FOLLOWING IN LINE

**Preparation**    The leader gives the dancers a rule for following a floor pattern. Here are some examples (shown in fig. 1):

- a. Travel in a curved path.
- b. Move parallel to the walls, making only right-angle turns.
- c. Travel along a spiral that starts at the outer edge of the space and ends in the center.
- d. Follow a sine wave that proceeds from one end of the space to the other, gradually decreasing in amplitude.

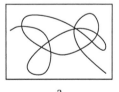

   a            b            c            d

**Figure 1**

**Procedures**    1. One dancer is first, with the others in a line behind, as in "follow the leader." The first dancer leads the group along the described path. Dancers walk or travel at an easy running pace. They may add some minimal body design motivated by the floor pattern, such as leaning around curves or exaggerating sudden changes in direction.

2. Each dancer devises a rule. Dancers then take turns leading the line according to their rule.

If the other dancers aren't told the rule, can they follow it just as well? Can they tell what it is?

Some patterns have their own endings. Otherwise, the leader calls an ending.

**Observation**    This problem helps the dancers conceptualize floor patterns, especially as a way to structure a sequence of movement from a beginning to an end.

### SPATIAL DEVICES

**Procedure**    All the dancers begin off the space. One dancer enters, using any locomotor movement, and travels through the space with attention to her floor pattern. One at a time other dancers enter the space, relating their floor patterns to that of the rest of the moving dancers. Dancers may enter or leave at any time. The first person who entered does not necessarily remain a leader. She may begin to follow another dancer's variation. All the dancers, however, should work toward creating one or two cohesive spatial patterns at any given time.

**Observations**    An experienced group may not need any further instructions. Even so, a discussion of the devices the dancers used will give them a common repertory of spatial relationships. The group should identify at least these basic relationships: following in line; traveling in parallel (same floor pattern in near or distant spatial relation); traveling in symmetry; reorienting the floor pattern in the space; decreasing or expanding the size of the floor pattern; repeating only part of someone else's pattern (see fig. 2).

The dancers should notice as well that repetition or repeated variations of patterns help the others relate to what is going on.

**Variations**    For beginners, limiting the movement to walking and running may allow them to focus more easily on the floor patterns. If they do not come up with most of the basic devices through their improvising, these devices can be named and the group can try them one by one.

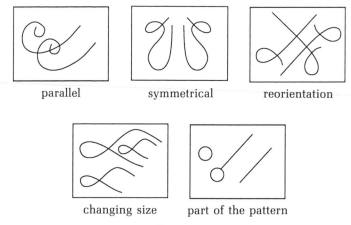

Figure 2

### RELATING TO A MOVING FIGURE

**Procedure**    The dancers divide into pairs. One dancer in each pair chooses a fixed path to follow. This might be a straight line, a circle, a figure 8, a square, a triangle, or some combination of straight lines and curves that can be repeated.

One duet at a time is in the space. The first dancer repetitively follows the fixed path. The partner may move anywhere in the space, relating his location and floor pattern to those of the first dancer. A systematic relationship is often the most visually effective, including symmetry, following in line, repetition of part of the pattern, and following the same pattern in another part of the space.

Beginners may wish to limit their movement to walking. Others may use any movement, but the movement of the two dancers should be related.

All dancers should have a turn at both roles.

**Variation**    In groups of three or four, one dancer has a set path, to which the others respond.

**Observations**    Since sharp direction changes create a different effect from curved paths, dancers can achieve more defined contrasts in the use of the space if the original floor pattern includes both angles and curves.

Dancers may find it difficult to be inventive with movement while focusing on their path. On the other hand, not too much movement invention is needed to complement interesting spatial relationships.

### DISCOVERING THE FLOOR PATTERN

**Preparation**  The leader devises a rule to limit the floor pattern. Here are some examples (shown in fig. 3):

    a. Travel counterclockwise around the space.

    b. Travel in straight lines, diagonally in the space, making right angle turns.

    c. Move only on the radii of a circle whose center is in the middle of the space.

Rules with two different conditions are more difficult:

    d. Move in straight paths in a given half of the space, and in curved paths in the other half.

The rule should be transmitted to no more than one third of the dancers. (This can be done by distributing a piece of paper to each dancer. Some pieces of paper contain the rule; others have some other message, so that everyone takes a moment to read. Or, more informally, the leader can whisper to each dancer, conveying the rule to some and to others another message.)

After a few run-throughs, a dancer may volunteer to devise a rule.

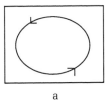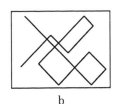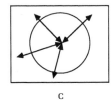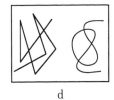

      a                    b                    c                    d

**Figure 3**

**Procedure**  All the dancers move freely within the space. The dancers knowing the rule must follow it consistently. The rest of the dancers move continuously as well. All the dancers relate to each other as much as they can. The aim of the problem is to have everyone eventually moving in accordance with the rule. This sometimes may occur even if not every dancer has consciously perceived the pattern.

To end, the leader may interrupt either when everyone is moving in accordance with the rule, or when no resolution seems forthcoming after a long time.

**Observation**   This problem has a nice moment of discovery as the casual interactions among the dancers evolve into a definite spatial pattern.

### GROUP FLOOR PATTERNS

**Procedure**   A group of no more than eight or ten dancers is in the space, each dancer in a still position.

One dancer at a time begins to move, with attention to his floor pattern. As each dancer begins to move, he should relate his floor pattern to those of the other dancers.

The goal is to evolve clear, visually interesting floor patterns among the group. The dancers may evolve one clear floor pattern, to which they all adhere, or they may divide into two or more groups, relating the floor patterns of the groups to each other.

The dancers can keep in mind the relationships they've already explored, such as moving close together as a group or following in line. They may also mirror one another. Some could move in a regular pattern, while others elaborate on that pattern. The dancers could also keep in mind the specific floor patterns they have already explored, including curved and straight paths, and covering large and small areas.

To enhance the visibility of the floor patterns, the dancers should use relatively simple movement and should imitate each other to a great extent.

On the first try, the dancers may briefly establish a pattern and soon find an ending. In successive tries, they may proceed through various transformations of the floor patterns and group relationships before finding an ending.

## DISTANCE

Dancers in technique class are used to jockeying for space, adjusting where they stand so that they have room enough to move. Dancers in performance, however, may sometimes be spaced close to or far from each other. These choreographic choices have formal consequences, shaping the space by the distribution of dancers; they also have dramatic effects, communicating something about human relationships by the proximity of dancers to each other.

In their daily lives people sense whether their distance from other people is appropriate to the circumstances. When they have an intimate conversation across a wide table, they lean forward. When a stranger gets too close they back off. In dance, where relationships are representational, dancers can learn to sense the import of their distances from one another and to use this sense to control the effect they make.

## MILLING

**Procedures** All the dancers stand together in a tight group in the space.

1. *Staying close.* Without using their hands to connect, the dancers stay close together and mill about while traveling as much as possible. The leadership and direction should change frequently and spontaneously. Any dancers who find themselves separating from the group should rejoin it, unless it immediately comes to follow them.

Dancers should take small, rapid steps to avoid stepping on anyone else's feet, and make quick changes of direction.

2. *Expanding and contracting.* The dancers mill about, staying close, as above. At the leader's cue, the group expands to fill the space, distributing themselves evenly throughout the space. The dancers should take larger steps, keep a lively pace, and travel throughout the space.

At the leader's cue, the group again contracts to the tight configuration and continues to travel as a group, taking small steps. The leader continues alternating the cues, varying the time spent close and distant. As this movement quickly becomes tiring, it shouldn't go on too long.

3. *Expanding and contracting without cues.* Beginning close together, the dancers mill about, expanding and contracting by group sense, without cues from the leader. They need not limit themselves to filling the space or being shoulder to shoulder. They may establish an intermediate distance, as long as it is consistent throughout the group. For example, they may expand, partly contract, and expand again before fully contracting.

The group should try not to be consistent in the length of time they spend at each distance. Changes of distance should be initiated by watching, rather than by a measured sense of timing. Unpredictability will demand total attention within the group.

## CENTER

**Procedure**   Preferably in a large space, the dancers are scattered throughout the space. One dancer is designated the "center" to begin. Each dancer takes note of his distance from the center.

The center may not move from his location, but performs circular movements in place. The other dancers move through the space, each one maintaining his original distance from the center. In this way, each dancer moves along the perimeter of a circle and all the dancers' circles are concentric. If a dancer encounters an obstacle, such as a wall, he must reverse direction. He may not shrink his circle in order to slip by. A dancer may reverse direction at any time. Dancers may only walk or run.

At any moment, another dancer may call out "Center." Without moving from her spot, the new center should make circular movements with her arms, legs, head, or torso, so that the others can easily recognize her as center. Each dancer should immediately observe his distance from the new center and, without stopping, move on a new circular path.

As this procedure goes on, individuals should call out "Center" more and more often, so that the dancers must adjust quickly.

The overall spatial design that results from this movement pattern will have the greatest range if succeeding centers are far from one another. The dancers may consider this as they choose when and where to become the center.

**Variation**   Each center establishes a movement motif which the others imitate or vary as they travel in their circles.

**Observations**   Some dancers will gravitate toward the center because that is where they are looking. Practice in overcoming this will help them be able to relate to dancers at a variety of distances.

Dancers can use this problem as a means to play with rearranging the distribution of dancers in the space.

## WALKING DUETS: DISTANCE

**Preparation**   The dancers walk randomly through the space, meeting the eyes of the other dancers as they pass. When they have all seen each other, the dancers gravitate toward a partner and continue to walk, in pairs. When they see that everyone is paired, they all stop.

**Procedures**    1. The dancers walk in pairs, staying close to their partners.

2. The pairs walk, starting close, but separating and coming back together intermittently.

3. The dancers walk. One person in each pair tries to avoid the other, while the other tries to stay close. After a minute or two, reverse roles.

**Observation**    By regulating only distance, the dancers' speed, focus, and emotional state can be affected. For example, the third procedure usually causes a form of hysteria.

### CHOOSING A DISTANCE

**Preparation**    Half the group is in the space. Each dancer looks around and chooses one other dancer and decides on a distance to try to maintain relative to that person: close, medium, or far.

**Procedure**    The dancers move freely in the space, trying to maintain their decided distances. One minute is a long enough time to discover and establish the relationship. Past one minute, stamina can become an issue for some choices.

Repeat the procedure several times, alternating groups. Different combinations of choices will produce very different results, from chaos to cohesion.

**Observations**    The dancers who are watching can observe what sorts of patterns of space and speed arise. Can they also figure out what combination of choices causes them?

## FOCUS

It is said that the eyes are windows to the soul. People react to the power of someone's gaze, especially if they feel it directed at them personally. Performers can create dramatic and emotive effects just by the use of their focus. Yvonne Rainer considered this an "artifice of performance," and chose to defy it in *Trio A*, where she never let the performers' gaze confront the audience.

Although live performance takes place in a real space, the audience's perception and understanding of the space goes beyond the literal arena in which the performance occurs. This imagined or abstract space is defined at least in part by the performers' use of focus.

Near and distant focus are explored here, for both their dramatic and spatial effects; other ways to use focus are explored in the chapter on Movement Invention.

### WALKING DUETS: FOCUS

**Procedures**  Pairs of dancers are in the space.

1. Each dancer walks anywhere in the space, keeping his focus continuously on his partner. Stillness is allowed.

2. Each dancer walks anywhere in the space, never looking at his partner. The focus may wander, dart, be fixed elsewhere, and so forth. Stillness is allowed.

3. The dancers walk in the space. One dancer in each pair looks continuously at his partner, while the partner always looks elsewhere. Stillness is allowed.

Reverse roles.

**Observations**  The use of focus will affect the attitudes of the partners to each other. It will also affect their spatial relationships: the paths they follow and their distance from each other.

In one of my classes a very short woman paired up with a very tall man. In procedure 3, they remained close to each other. She looked at him constantly, actively trying to get him to look at her. He stayed totally cool and looked all around. He could see right over her head.

### WALKING DUETS: DISTANCE AND FOCUS

**Preparation**  Pairs of dancers are in the space. Each dancer silently chooses whether to keep her focus on her partner or never look at her partner, and whether to stay close or keep at a distance.

**Procedure**  The dancers walk in the space, each one trying to maintain her chosen focus and distance.

**Variation**  If at some point a dancer feels the need to change, she may change her focus or distance, or both. This may be done only once by any dancer in any given run-through. The leader should allow enough time for the dancers to change their relationship before calling an end.

**Observations**   Clearly, the relationships are easier to maintain when both partners choose the same distance. The changes made during the variation usually aim to establish more stable relationships, though a few will always prefer the challenge of the conflict.

Without any named dramatic intent, the simple choices of focus and distance tend to create dramatic relationships between the partners.

### THREE FOCUSES I

**Procedures**   All the dancers are in the space, standing still.

1. Keeping their focus close to their own bodies, the dancers explore the range of movement that is spontaneously motivated by this focus. Dancers may relate to others whom they perceive with their peripheral vision.

2. The focus is on real entities in the space: the walls, floor, furniture, fixtures, and the other dancers. As they move, the dancers should react to what they see in the room. They may touch things or imitate their shapes. They relate to the other dancers, using imitation, variation, and contrast. They may consider space, design, and rhythm.

Dancers may need a reminder to move large or fast, and to take their movement down to the floor or up in the air.

Spend as much time as necessary on this phase, as it has many possibilities.

3. The focus is on the far distance: the moon, the horizon, the center of the earth. The ceiling, walls, or floor need not restrict this gaze. The dancers explore the range of movement suggested by this focus. They may relate to others whom they perceive with their peripheral vision.

**Observations**   This problem helps the dancers be aware of their focus, so that it can't, for example, remain inward.

It also offers a context for developing the habit of paying attention to the other dancers. No result is solicited, just the seeing. Surprising interactions almost inevitably arise.

### THREE FOCUSES II

**Procedure**   This problem has three phases. It begins with the dancers standing around the edge of the space.

In phase one, the dancers enter individually, keeping their focus close to themselves and moving accordingly.

At any time, dancers may choose to go on to phase two, focusing on the room and on the other dancers. They move accordingly and relate their movement to what they see. Gradually all the dancers join this phase.

Phase two should continue for a while, allowing for response to the many stimuli in this range.

At any time, the dancers may go on to phase three: distant focus. This focus tends to isolate the dancers. They may, however, allow themselves to react to the other dancers insofar as they perceive them peripherally.

To end, each dancer comes to a still position when he chooses, until all are still.

### THREE FOCUSES III

**Procedure**  To begin, the dancers make a group composition of still shapes.

The dancers may at any time choose any of the three focuses: close, middle, or distant, and move accordingly. They may change when they wish. At all times they should be perfectly clear which focus they are using.

The dancers should be aware of each other and develop this problem as a group.

When the dancers sense that they have sufficiently explored the problem, one at a time they may take a still shape. Dancers should be prepared to hold their final positions for a long time, until everyone is still.

## LOCATION

Do the dancers control the space, or does the space control the dancers? Are there areas that have their own characteristics: formality or intimacy, strength or weakness? Doris Humphrey believed so. Traditional ballet used the space according to set criteria. Can the ambience of certain areas be overruled by reorganizing the space with the focus or distribution of the dancers? Merce Cunningham believed so and chose to give all areas equal value.

The following problems explore how effects are created by the location of the dancers relative to the space and relative to each other.

Three Focuses III. Two dancers with inward focus and one with distant focus.

### LOCATION AFFECTS MOVEMENT

**Procedure**    All the dancers begin in the space. The leader acts as the audience, at one end of the space. From time to time dancers may join the leader for a little while, to observe and to give more of a sense of audience presence.

The dancers move freely in various areas of the space. They should spend some time in the center, near the walls or borders of the space, upstage and downstage, and in the corners. They should explore particular areas, such as platforms or alcoves, if there are any. The dancers should allow the location to affect their movement. In particular, they should remain aware of the presence of the audience and the stage space as it relates to the audience.

**Variation**    Only one dancer at a time is in the space. All the others are observers.

**Observation**    In what ways does location affect the size, design, focus, energy, and mood of the movement? This may not be the same for different dancers.

### FOCAL POINTS

**Preparation**    The leader chooses two spots on the floor, which everyone can identify and locate.

**Procedure**    One at a time, dancers enter and move in the space. They mentally focus on the two spots and let this motivate where they travel and where they spend time in the space. They may feel drawn to the spots, or repelled, but should avoid a literal, dramatic rendering of their responses.

**Focal Points**

The dancers should also respond to the location of the other dancers in the space.

Repeat this with different spots.

**Variations**    1. A dancer may be placed on each spot. They may either remain still or respond, in place, to the movement around them.

2. Dancers will work with only one spot, which, however, will not be identified beforehand. The group must gravitate to some spot and mutually, silently agree on where it is, and then continue to respond to it as their focal point.

**Observation**    Because of the definite, common focus, the problem encourages strong group interaction.

### LOCATION FOR FOUR DANCERS

**Preparation**    The dancers divide into groups of four. Each group will decide on a way to divide the space so that the entire area is accounted for and each dancer has his own area that no one else may enter. They should take into consideration the placement of the audience.

Examples (shown in fig. 4) include: (a) four strips of space from one side to the other; (b) four quadrants; (c) four diagonal areas; and (d) a central circle enclosed by three areas.

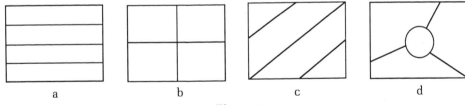

a                  b                  c                  d

**Figure 4**

**Procedure**    One quartet at a time is in the space. The four dancers move, each one traveling within his area. Stillness is allowed. Dancers should always pay attention to where they are relative to each other, as seen by the audience. They may consider the distances between themselves, their location in the space, and the direction of travel relative to the space and to each other.

**Observations**    Do the dancers manage to create relationships appropriate to the division of the space? Are some divisions of the space more effective than others? Why?

# GROUPINGS

Related to distance and location, groupings direct the dancers toward an awareness of their spatial arrangements. Avoiding any concern with body design, the problems that follow, in their austere simplicity, focus the dancers on the possibility of generating exciting improvisations through the manipulation of only their placement and traveling in the space.

## STATIONARY CONFIGURATIONS

**Procedures**    The dancers begin off the space. In each of the three procedures they enter the space one at a time and stand still, using no additional body design. They will create stationary configurations according to various instructions.

1. The leader names a familiar figure for the group to make: a circle, a square, an S, a T, a figure 8, a V, a straight line, or a triangle. Dancers may suggest other configurations.

The dancers should also pay attention to their facing. They can try more than one arrangement of facings for any given configuration and see how the facings affect the design.

2. Without predetermining what it will be, the dancers create a familiar figure by observing the gradually emerging design.

3. The dancers make nongeometrical distributions of bodies in space, including clusters and scattering. These figures should be just as strong and specific in their own right as were the familiar figures.

At the end of each configuration, the dancers should leave the space one at a time, with attention to the new configurations that appear as some dancers leave.

**Variation**    Repeat the procedures, with the dancers free to assume any body design when they enter the space. The body designs should be related to each other.

### A MOVING CONFIGURATION

**Procedures**    1. A group of at least five dancers arranges itself in a line in the space. Keeping the line formation, the group moves through the space. The dancers' facings within the line may change, to help them in their travels. The line may move as a rank, or as a column; it may rotate around any of the dancers as the pivotal point. It can move parallel to the walls or obliquely.

2. The dancers may evolve their line into other configurations that they formed in Stationary Configurations. These configurations may move through the space, though they need not. Stillness will be helpful.

**Observations**    In this problem concentration is needed to achieve a simple result. Mastery of this difficulty will help produce clear and exciting results in faster paced or more complex grouping problems, such as the last two in this section.

### EVOLVING GROUPINGS

**Procedure**    All the dancers start outside the space. One at a time they walk into the space and stand still, gradually forming groupings by their location relative to each other.

Dancers may enter and leave the space when they wish, always with their focus on creating, changing, and disbanding groupings. Dancers may not change places while in the space. They may, however, leave and reenter immediately. Dancers should aim to spend about half the time in the space and half the time watching.

Dancers should not leave the space too soon after entering. It is essential that they allow the other dancers time to see the formations and to react before these have changed.

Entrances and exits should be as simple and unadorned as possible, as should be the stance in the space. Attention should be uniquely on location and groupings.

### WALKING, RUNNING, AND STILLNESS

**Procedure**    The dancers begin off the space. One dancer at a time enters the space and stands still, relating to the arrangement of dancers already in the space, as in the last problem. This continues until all have entered the space.

The dancers now may walk or run, at any speed, or be still. As in the last problem, they will pay attention to the groupings that are formed, both by the stationary dancers and by the moving dancers.

In addition, they should work for rhythmic clarity within the group, playing off the pulse and accents of each other's movement. Repetition will help keep the rhythmic element simple and cohesive.

Dancers may wish to move in unison with someone else, either close to them or at a distance.

The dancers can try to create variety in the design, energy, and rhythmic character of succeeding sections: some densely clustered, some sparse, some symmetrical, some with geometric configurations, some slow, some fast, some mixed. The generous use of stillness will help focus this problem.

### ENTRANCES AND EXITS

**Procedure**  This should be done on a stage, or a space should be organized to create a stage area, so that the dancers know which direction is front. The leader should sit in the audience, and one or more dancers at a time may sit out to join the audience. The dancers begin in the wings, or off to the sides of the stage area.

Dancers may enter the space, move or be still, and leave, at their own discretion. There should be variety in the number of dancers entering, onstage, and leaving at various times. There should be variety in the groupings that they form. There can be solos; there can be one or more clearly defined groups; there can be a mob. Several dancers might enter in unison, but stay or leave in diverse ways.

The piece ends when all the dancers leave and no one enters after an appreciable pause.

## LEVELS

The improvisations in this chapter have so far been concerned primarily with the distribution of bodies in the space. One way to design those bodies and break up the visual space is to disrupt the purely horizontal axis of movement.

If the middle level range is our practical, everyday functional level, the higher and lower levels take us immediately into a new realm: the dramatic, the expressive, the stylized. In ballet the upper level predominates. In contrast, one of the goals of early modern dance was to give the lie to the effortlessness of ballet's verticality and reveal the effort of moving against gravity. One result was a great increase in the use of the low level.

The work that follows offers situations in which the dancers can explore the higher and lower levels and add these dimensions to their designing the group in space.

## FALLS

**Procedures** All the dancers are in the space.

1. The dancers individually explore ways to go down to the floor (which will be called falls, nothing involuntary implied) and to rise. They may begin with falls they have learned elsewhere, in technique classes, choreographed dances, or martial arts. Then they should make some falls of their own.

Falls may be sustained descents, slides, fast drops, to the side, forward, backward, diagonal, combined with a roll or a spiraling action. One can even jump into a fall. Dancers may be still at the bottom, continue smoothly through the fall to a rise, or rebound to rise.

To extend their repertory of falls, the dancers may also imitate what they see others doing.

2. With one dancer supporting the weight of another, pairs of dancers explore falls. This should be done without speaking or sign language. Dancers may teach each other falls they already know (from dance, wrestling, martial arts, gymnastics, etc.). This should be done with care for the safety of the dancers, preferably on mats.

One dancer may support the weight of another, or they may share weight so that both can descend together. They can also find ways to help one another to rise. This may include lifts.

Dancers may circulate and change partners.

**Observations** Different floor surfaces will assist and inhibit different kinds of falls. A smooth or slippery surface will allow dancers to slide; linoleum generally won't. A mat will cushion the impact of falls or rolls. A thin body may find painful what a well-padded body does comfortably.

### WALKING, RUNNING, AND FALLING

**Procedures**   All the dancers are in the space, working individually.

1. Each dancer walks in the space, goes down to the floor, and holds a position there. At their own time, dancers may rise and continue.

2. Dancers run in the space, go down to the floor quickly, immediately rise without stopping, and continue.

3. The leader keeps a pulse, to which dancers may either walk or run double-time. Dancers may either walk, go to the floor, hold still, and rise, or run, go to the floor, and rise without stopping. Dancers may change back and forth from the walking pace to the running pace whenever they wish.

Once the dancers are familiar with this activity, they should begin to relate to each other, considering the tempo and spacing of their traveling and falling, and the design of their falls.

**Walking, Running, and Falling**

### HIGH LEVEL

**Preparation**   The dancers name all the ways they can think of to move at a high level. These may include: platforms, ladders, stools, chairs, and the like, which place the dancer at a height; lifts assisted by one or more dancers; elevation movements including leaps (from one foot to the other), hops (from one foot to the same foot), and jumps (including all the remaining alternatives); and gestures or movements that reach overhead.

**Procedures**   1. The dancers individually explore a variety of movement at a high level that they can do alone or with props and sets.

2. Reviewing what they did in Weight Dependency in the chapter on Preliminaries, dancers walk in the space, gathering into duets, trios, and larger groups and explore ways to lift each other off the floor. They may also try assisted elevation movements, in which one person helps another to jump, leap, or hop high in the air. Under safe circumstances, one dancer may even be thrown through the air, to be caught by another, to land on her own feet, or to land and roll. Only if this can be done safely!

If a group of dancers needs more assistance, they may call out "Help," but otherwise should avoid talk as a means to direct cooperation.

### GROUP COMPOSITION WITH LEVELS

**Procedures**   All the dancers begin off the space.

1. One at a time the dancers enter, taking still shapes in the space, considering the location and shapes and levels of the other dancers in the space. Dancers may not change their shapes while in the space, but they may exit and reenter as they wish, to take a new shape.

2. The dancers may take still shapes in the space, or may travel through the space at any level. They may enter and exit. There should be no more than two events in the space at a time. Dancers should use a variety of levels to give interest to the group composition.

### TRAVELING WITH UPS AND DOWNS

**Procedure**   All the dancers start outside the space. They enter one at a time when they wish. They may leave and reenter the space at any time, as they judge appropriate.

When in the space, dancers may walk, run, fall, get up, and go up in the air. These movements may be done alone or with others, with or without assistance. Dancers may also be still, at any level. Stillness will complement the exertion of changing levels.

Dancers who have exited may accompany the movement with sound. This may be pulsed or non-pulsed. Dancers in the space may also include sound.

The space should not be cluttered with too much activity. Everyone should pay attention to the use of space in traveling, the distribution and design of the group, and the tempo and rhythms of the movement. With this awareness, the dancers should develop a group improvisation that has coherence in any one period and variety through time.

**Variation**    Dancers are not limited to walking and running as means of travel. Variants on traveling should be used to contribute to the group composition, rather than for variety.

**Observations**    Dancers should not lose the continuity of their performance when they change levels. They should maintain an awareness of the overall design of the group.

## GROUP DESIGN

Group design can be formal, like a marching band, or informal, like a family picnic. The more formal version often contains elements of unison or symmetry; the less formal is usually asymmetrically composed.

Although humans are built more or less symmetrically, they rarely find themselves in symmetrical positions. Sitting, people cross their legs or lean on an elbow; standing, they ease their weight into one hip; walking, they alternate from one leg to the other. Yet they often mirror the stance and gesture of the person they are talking to: both will stand with arms crossed, or chin in hand. In this way a symmetrical design is formed by the two figures together.

This sort of formality is not necessary for a sense of design, however. It can come equally well from asymmetrical groupings and attention to levels and body design.

In this section, the dancers will approach group design via both symmetry and asymmetry.

## SYMMETRICAL AND ASYMMETRICAL SHAPES

**Procedures**   1. The dancers are scattered throughout the space. The leader establishes a slow pulse, with clapping or music.

Each dancer strikes a shape that is symmetrical (with respect to the vertical plane dividing their right and left sides) on the first beat, and comes to "center," i.e., a simple upright stance, on the next beat. Dancers continue to alternate symmetrical shapes with center, changing on each beat. Each new shape is reached in one clear movement and held until the next clear change. The dancers should consider levels and the use of all parts of the body.

2. Dancers alternate taking asymmetrical shapes with coming to center, on the pulse.

3. The dancers divide into two equal groups: performers and audience. The performers place themselves in a grouping so that all are facing the audience and visible to them.

To a slow, steady pulse established by the leader or music, performers alternate individual, symmetrical shapes with individual, asymmetrical shapes, on the beat. Dancers need not relate to each other.

Change groups and repeat.

**Observations**   Did the audience perceive a different effect made by symmetrical and asymmetrical shapes?

Did any dancers use a systematic method to alternate between symmetrical and asymmetrical shapes? They may have changed their entire body shape every beat, or they may have adjusted half of the body from a symmetrical shape to an asymmetrical one. They may have discovered some surprising shapes by keeping half of an asymmetrical shape and adjusting the other half of the body to match it.

## SYMMETRICAL GROUP TABLEAUX

**Procedure**   The dancers are divided into two equal groups. They are all at one edge of the space, which will be the front. Until a dancer enters, she is part of the audience.

Any dancer from group one enters the space and takes a shape (which is not symmetrical). Anyone from group two enters and takes the symmetrically opposite shape, from the point of view of the audience at the

**Symmetrical Shapes**

**Asymmetrical Shapes**

front. One by one, all the dancers add themselves to the space in this manner, creating a tableau that is symmetrical relative to a central axis.

Group one dancers should consider the overall design when adding themselves to the space, including level and location as well as body shape. They should also make sure all the shapes are visible, and that dancers downstage don't block those upstage.

Group two dancers should make sure to center the symmetry in the space.

Repeat, reversing roles of the groups.

**Variation**    A few dancers may add themselves as solo symmetrical figures along the center line of the space.

## ADDITION AND SUBTRACTION

I learned this problem from Wendy Rogers, who learned it from Ruth Hatfield.

**Procedures**    In all four phases the dancers begin off the space. Dancers are free to choose when to enter the space and when to leave. These choices should be made by considering the composition and activity of the group in the space. Dancers shouldn't rush to enter. In general, they should spend about half the time watching and half the time in the space.

Any dancer in the space should stay long enough for the others to look and react. Before leaving, a dancer should consider whether he is still contributing to the overall group activity.

Even if the group is reduced to one or no dancers in the space at some moment, the improvisation need not end. If, however, no one chooses to enter soon, this is a good way to end each phase.

1. The dancers form static group compositions. To begin, one dancer walks into the space and takes a shape that can be held for a while. At any time other dancers may walk into the space and take still shapes that add to the sculptural design of the group. Body design, level, and location relative to others (including contact) should be considered.

Dancers may not change their shapes while in the space. They may, however, leave and return immediately if they want to.

The walk into and out of the space should be unadorned, used only to get into place. Each shape should be taken as simply and directly as possible.

2. The dancers perform repetitive, stationary movement, with sound. To begin, a dancer enters and performs a repetitive movement or short phrase of movement that does not take her through space. The timing as well as the design of the repetitions should be consistent. Dancers may use sound as well: percussive or vocal, including words. The sound must also remain consistent.

All dancers adding themselves to the space must perform stationary, repetitive movements. They should be aware of both the static group composition and the rhythmic relationships they establish. Dramatic or comic effects often arise in this phase, but should not obscure the spatial or rhythmic composition.

The dancers are reminded not to make changes while in the space. They may leave and reenter to make changes.

3. The dancers perform repetitive, traveling movement. This may be a single, repetitive movement or a short, repetitive phrase. They should consider stamina and choose movements they will be able to sustain. Dancers may not stay in one place. Sound may be included.

To enter, a dancer may either walk to a place and begin, or use a repetitive movement to enter; similarly, to exit.

This phase can easily become chaotic, with a diversity of movements, floor patterns, and rhythms. To avoid this, dancers should begin by using unison, or varying someone else's movement in only one way at a time. For example, a dancer might imitate another, but travel in the opposite direction; or she might follow along with another dancer, performing the same step with a different design in the arms.

4. The dancers may do all of the above. To begin, one dancer enters and takes a still shape. After this, dancers may add themselves to the space in any of the three ways explored.

Again, dancers should exit and reenter to make any change in what they are doing, even to add sound to a repetitive movement.

**Observations**   In this problem the dancers are asked to incorporate design, rhythm, and floor pattern progressively into the improvisation, so that it is a good exercise in integrating skills.

Because of the strict rules about entering and leaving the space, this problem helps the group learn about and practice the attentive observation and slow pacing that make any improvisation more coherent.

## SHAPE AND SHAPE SEQUENCES

Shape is present in all bodies, whether still or in motion. By stopping action and paying attention to the shapes their bodies take, the dancers can use shape as a device to play with rhythm and with the process of developing relationships in time. By adding movement back to their shapes, they have a fertile source of movement invention.

### INDIVIDUAL SHAPES

Procedure
All the dancers run easily through the space at random, meeting the eyes of all the other dancers as they pass.

At any time, a dancer quickly stops and takes a shape. In quick succession, the other dancers stop and take shapes. They may be close together or scattered through the space. The shapes may be taken in relation to others or not.

Once everyone is still there is a brief pause, and the dancers again resume running. Any dancer may initiate the next group shape.

Observations
Some dancers may find they take similar shapes each time. What characterizes these shapes? Try the procedure again to extend the range of responses.

### HAND DIALOGUES

Procedures
1. *Still hand shapes.* Dancers are in pairs, standing facing their partners. One dancer in each pair takes a shape with his hands. The other dancer takes a shape with her hands in response. The first dancer responds to this with another hand shape. This process continues, with the dancers alternating changes.

A dancer may use one hand or both hands. She may change the shape of her hands, or may move them to a different point in space, or both. Each change should be made in one clear movement and then held. Dancers should try to establish a motif and develop it for a while before evolving a new motif.

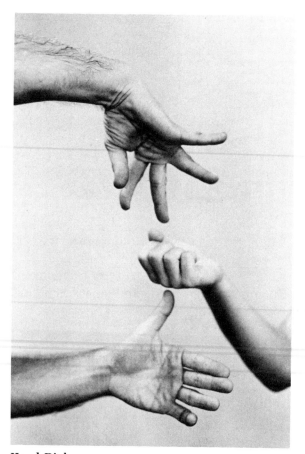

**Hand Dialogues**

When pairs have spent some time in this dialogue, they may take turns showing their work to the rest of the group. If they have a favorite sequence of changes, this should be included in the showing.

2. *Moving the hands.* Pairs of dancers relate both the shape and movement of their hands to each other's. They need not take turns, but may keep moving, always reacting to each other. Movement is still restricted to the hands only. Stillness may be included.

3. *Still body shapes initiated by hands.* Using the hands to initiate changes of shape in the whole body, pairs of dancers create a succession of still shapes. Here too, they should develop one motif at a time, rather than seek variety.

4. *Body movements initiated by hands.* Pairs of dancers create an on-going interaction of whole body movements initiated by their hands. Stillness may be included.

**Variation**    Repeat the procedures using another part of the body: shoulders, feet, face, and so on.

**Observations**    Different types of development may be used by the various pairs of dancers: imitation, variation, contrast, question and answer.

A range of relationships, expressions, or attitudes may arise between partners.

This problem usually generates a quiet, intense concentration, even for beginners.


### QUARTETS: TAKING SHAPES

**Procedure**    All the dancers are in the space, divided into quartets, consisting of dancers A, B, C, and D.

Dancer A takes a shape. B takes a shape in relation to A's shape. C takes a shape in relation to the shape of the duet AB. D is looking on. A leaves. B and C stay. D takes a shape in relation to the shape of this duet. Schematically we have:

$$
\begin{array}{l}
A \\
A\ B \\
A\ B\ C \\
\phantom{A\ }B\ C \\
\phantom{A\ }B\ C\ D \\
\phantom{A\ B\ }C\ D \\
\phantom{A\ B\ }C\ D\ A
\end{array}
$$

This rotation of duets and trios continues, allowing each dancer a moment to look and decide on a shape, and to watch the shapes evolve.

The dancers should pay attention to the evolution of the sculpture through time, rather than seek unique individual shapes. They may choose to imitate another's shape exactly, or to vary level, direction, or focus. They may sometimes be close and sometimes distant.

Once the quartets have developed an ease in working together, each group shows a sequence of shapes to the rest of the dancers.

**Variation**    Repeat with groups of five or more, always with one dancer rotating out to observe, as above.

**Observations**    How did each group develop its shape sequence? By repetition? Variation? Contrast? Use of space? Were all of these means successful?

### WAVES OF MOVEMENT

**Procedure**    Six dancers are in the space. Each dancer is assigned his own count, from one to six. The dancers begin close together, in a static group composition. Slow, eight-count phrases are established using music, counting, clapping, or a metronome.

The dancers will move in the following counted pattern:

```
Dancer 1:  1  2  3  (still)  •  •  •   1  2  3  •  •
Dancer 2:  •  2  3  4  (still)  •  •  •   2  3  4  •
Dancer 3:  •  •  3  4  5  (still)  •  •  •   3  4  5
Dancer 4:  •  •  •  4  5  6  (still)  •  •  •  etc.
Dancer 5:  •  •  •  •  5  6  7  (still)  •  •  etc.
Dancer 6:  •  •  •  •  •  6  7  8  (still)  •  etc.
```

Each dancer moves for three counts, beginning on his assigned count, and otherwise is still. In this way there are waves of movement beginning on count one and ending on count eight.

A dancer's movement may be either sustained or accented. Dancers should relate the design of their movement and their still shapes to the design formed by the rest of the group. Level, direction, and angularity should be considered. The dancers need not stay close together, but should continue to relate to the design of the whole group, even at a distance.

**Variation**    Eliminate the counts. The dancers are assigned a sequential order, so that each one knows whom to follow. The first dancer begins to move. At any time after this the second dancer may begin to move. The third dancer may begin any time after the second, and so forth. Dancers need not rush to begin. A dancer may choose to wait until all other movement has stopped before starting her turn. Any number of dancers may be moving at a time. Dancers may stop whenever they choose to. The phrasing of the group movement should not become too even. Surges of movement may contrast with quiet moments.

The space shouldn't get too cluttered with movement. All movement should aim to enhance the group design, both moving and stationary.

**Observations**  Especially in the uncounted variation, dancers may need to take care in their choice of still positions at the end of their movement, so that they are able to see the rest of the group.

Some groups may do better with the limitation of the set counts; others may prefer the freedom of choosing their own timing.

### SHAPE CANON

**Preparation**  All the dancers are in the space. They learn the following instructions for eight four-count phrases:

| Phrase | Movement |
|---|---|
| 1 | Run 8 steps (double time) |
| 2 | Continue to run, 8 more steps (double time) |
| 3 | Take a shape on count one and hold it |
| 4 | Melt out of that shape by moving slowly 4 counts |
| 5 | Take another shape on count one and hold it |
| 6 | Keep holding it |
| 7 | Keep holding it |
| 8 | Melt out of this shape |

The leader sets a pace that is half the speed of comfortable running steps. All together, the dancers practice moving according to this sequence of instructions. They should take their shapes cleanly and exactly on count one.

**Procedure**  The dancers are divided into two groups, and all are in the space. They will perform the phrase they just practiced, but in canon.

The leader sets a pulse. All the dancers begin to move at the same time, at a cue from the leader. Dancers in group one will begin with the fifth phrase, taking a shape and holding it. Dancers in group two will run double-time for two phrases, mingling among the other group's shapes and looking for one to imitate. On count one of the third phrase, each dancer from group two imitates a shape made by one of the dancers in group one, and holds for the rest of the phrase. Then all melt out of the shape during the fourth phrase.

Now the roles are reversed. Group two dancers take a shape and hold, while group one dancers run, choose a shape, and imitate it. All the dancers melt during the last phrase, and the cycle begins anew. Schematically, it looks like this:

| Phrase | Group 1 | Group 2 |
|--------|---------|---------|
| 1 | Take a shape | Run 8 steps |
| 2 | Hold | Run 8 steps |
| 3 | Hold | Imitate someone's shape |
| 4 | Melt | Melt |
| 5 | Run 8 steps | Take a shape |
| 6 | Run 8 steps | Hold |
| 7 | Imitate someone's shape | Hold |
| 8 | Melt | Melt |

The beauty of this problem depends on accuracy in the timing. Dancers should take their shapes clearly on count one; the others begin to run at the same moment.

For overall design considerations, dancers should get close to the dancer whose shape they are imitating, so that there are clusters of identical shapes. It is best if the different shapes aren't located too close together.

Dancers should vary the types of shape they take each time. Their shapes may be open, closed, curved, angular, high, middle, low, vertical, horizontal, or diagonal.

**Variations**    1. Instead of imitating the shapes that they see, dancers may respond to them with a related shape, still getting close to the shape they are relating to.

2. For the fourth and eighth phrases, instead of melting out of the shape, dancers may move in ways inspired by the shape.

**Observations**    This problem can be used effectively in a technique class to introduce several concepts in a simple way: awareness of shapes, group design, and accuracy in timing. Because it fits so easily into a technique class format, it is a good introduction to improvisation and can bypass the students' potential for self-consciousness.

## MOVING A SHAPE

**Procedures**    1. *Solos.* Each dancer chooses a static shape. It need not be elaborate or unusual.

All the dancers are in the space, working individually. Each one explores the movement possibilities inherent in the shape he's chosen. The shape may be taken into the air or down to the floor. An impulse in part of the body may initiate movement. Dancers may turn in the shape, or travel it through space.

All movement will cause some deviation from the original shape. The dancers should begin by being as true as possible to the original shape. They may then go on to explore possibilities of changing part of the shape while keeping other parts intact.

Dancers then take turns showing some of the results of their exploration.

2. *Small or moderate-sized groups.* Each group, together with the leader, chooses one of the shapes from the first procedure that seemed to be a good source of movement.

With this shape as the basis, the dancers improvise as a group, isolating one movement motivation at a time: level, impulse, turning, and traveling. Stillness should be included. Dancers should pay attention to the group design, both static and moving, and to the rhythmic relationships created by their movement.

Each group should decide on one of the motivations that worked well with their shape and show a short improvisation to the other dancers.

## MOVING A SERIES OF SHAPES

**Procedure**  A group of three to five dancers chooses an order among themselves, first through third (fourth, fifth). They place themselves in the space, standing so that all can see the first dancer.

The first dancer takes a shape. The others imitate the shape exactly, until all are still. One at a time, they begin to move, using the shape to motivate their movement, relating to each other as a group.

The second dancer, when he chooses, takes a new shape. One at a time the other dancers move into this shape, until all are still. One at a time, the dancers begin to move, until they all are improvising together on this shape.

This repeats until all the dancers have initiated a shape. Movement into and out of the shapes should not break the continuity of the performance.

The dancers have the opportunity of intermingling the various ways of moving a shape that they've practiced in Moving a Shape. They should use this freedom to work for group coherence in each section. They should

**Moving a Series of Shapes**

aim for contrast from section to section: in the design of the shapes, in the energy and rhythms of the movement generated by the shapes, and in duration.

To end, any dancer repeats the shape he took in his turn. Each dancer soon takes his own original shape, with attention to the final group composition, until all the dancers are still.

### MOVING A SHAPE: DUETS

Procedure   The dancers divide into pairs. Some of the pairs are in the space, and some are audience.

One dancer in each pair takes a shape and holds it. The other dancer takes a shape in response. The two dancers then have a movement dialogue, each one moving as motivated by her shape, while also relating to her partner. Some attentive stillness is helpful, though dancers need not take turns moving.

The way the movement dialogue develops will depend largely on the original shapes: whether they are similar or contrasting.

These duets may be brief, aiming to develop the relationship succinctly and clearly. Dancers should find an ending in stillness.

Repeat this procedure, with the second dancer now choosing the initial shape. The first dancer then responds with a shape, aiming to suggest a different relationship between the two shapes than they had in the first duet.

**Observation**    Sometimes a dramatic situation arises in a duet. In cases where this happens, does it enhance or inhibit the movement interest?

## TRACE DESIGNS

In the 1970s, Michael Moschen of the Big Apple Circus revived the art of juggling flaming torches. In a darkened hall, the movement of the fire left traces drawn in the air. This was accompanied by the whoosh of the flames and the periodic illumination of the performer's arms and chest as the fire passed over, around, and across his body. Dancers can hardly hope to achieve such a dramatic manifestation of trace design. However, they can leave traces by wearing light colors against a dark background, or by moving so sculpturally that they inscribe their movements in the viewer's imagination.

### VOLUMES I

**Procedures**    1. The leader describes a volume of space. This could be a large box two feet high by three feet wide by fifteen feet long, or a six-foot sphere, or a four-inch cube.

Working individually, each dancer locates and defines this volume by his movement, using all parts of his body, not just hands. A dancer may choose to be inside or outside of the volume.

2. The leader describes a large volume of space, for example a pyramid with a square base, eight feet to a side, and eight feet high. As a group, the dancers will define this volume.

The dancers begin off the space. One dancer enters and begins to locate and define the volume in space. One at a time the other dancers enter, moving with an awareness of the exact location and shape of the volume, and helping to define the volume with their movement.

**Observations**    Some difficulties may come up. The dancers may not all agree on the location, shape, and size of the volume. They may have a problem going from outside to inside the volume and back out. How do the dancers solve this? Or do they avoid it? The use of mime can come to dominate the movement. How can this be avoided?

## VOLUMES II

**Preparation**    Each dancer chooses a volume. It may be regular, irregular, smooth, jagged, geometrical, small, large, low, or tall. The dancer should define it precisely in her imagination. It will help to use an image, such as a giant egg carton, or a cluster of rocks.

**Procedure**    One at a time the dancers move, defining the volume in space so that the audience can see it.

**Observations**    Can the audience describe the volume defined? Was any sense of texture or solidity created? For example, does a rock look different from a similarly shaped sponge?

## VOLUMES III

**Procedure**    All the dancers are at one end of the space. A steady pulse is established using music or clapping. Two or three dancers at a time move across the space. They run eight steps, then enclose a volume of space with part of their bodies: for example, with an arm and the torso, or a leg and an arm. They change the shape of this volume for the second eight counts, allowing it to grow, shrink, or change in contour. The second line of dancers then starts into the space, while the first line repeats the runs and shapes as many times as it takes to travel across the space.

## INDIVIDUAL TRACE DESIGNS

**Procedures**    1. All the dancers are in the space, working individually. They trace designs in the air using one part of the body at a time: finger, elbow, nose, shoulder, hip, knee, foot. They may move through the space. They should be aware of the cumulative trace designs in time.

2. All the dancers move individually in space, considering the trace design created by the whole body.

3. Each dancer chooses one part of the body with which to trace a design. One at a time the dancers create trace designs for the rest of the group.

## CIRCLES AND STRAIGHT LINES

**Preparations**    All the dancers are in the space. Dancers will create designs in space by four means: static shapes, trace designs with a part of the body, floor pattern, and configuration of dancers.

1. *Static shapes.* Working individually and using static shape, dancers find as many ways as they can to form circles, using all or part of the body. Repeat this, forming straight lines.

2. *Trace designs.* Moving individually, dancers find ways to trace circles and straight lines by moving a part of the body in space. The trace designs may lie in any plane: vertical, horizontal, or oblique.

3. *Floor pattern.* Moving individually, dancers trace small and large circles and straight lines by their floor patterns. Any movement is allowed.

4. *Configuration of dancers.* The dancers stand in a circle. They move through the space, trying to keep the circle. Repeat this with a straight line.

**Procedure**    If the group is large enough, half the dancers may watch while the other half dances.

The dancers begin in a circle, each one forming a circle or straight line with some part of his body.

The dancers move, always creating a circle or a straight line by one of the four means just practiced. Two or more dancers may work together in some instances to create a static shape.

Dancers should be aware of the entire group. At some time they may all shape circles, at another time all shape straight lines. Or they may divide into two groups, one using circles, the other using straight lines, and carry on a movement dialogue between the groups. They should always pay attention to the design of the whole group.

## MOCK ORANGE

**Preparations**    Considering a circle as the letter *O* and a straight line as the letter *I*, the dancers can extend their work in Circles and Straight Lines and form any letter of the alphabet in several ways.

1. *Static shapes.* Dancers explore ways of shaping the letters of the alphabet with their bodies. The letters may be print or script, upper case or lower case. Dancers may make shapes with their whole bodies, or with only parts: hands, mouth, arms, and so on.

The leader calls out letters, with the dancers trying to find several ways to shape each letter. The leader may also call out a word, with the dancers going from one shape to the next, using a variety of body parts.

2. *Trace designs.* Dancers trace letters by moving a part of the body in the air. This should not move through the space, except as the result of tracing.

Again, the leader may start by calling out letters, then words, for the dancers to trace. When spelling a whole word, dancers may use different parts of the body to trace different letters.

3. *Floor pattern.* Dancers travel so that their floor pattern traces the letters. They may move however they wish, as long as they trace the letter on the floor. Dancers may suggest letters and words to use for practice.

4. *Combining methods.* With the leader or dancers calling out words to spell, the dancers may combine any of the three spelling techniques, making sure to use only one at a time. At first, dancers may need to pause between letters when making the transition from one mode of spelling to another. They eventually should be able to make these transitions without a pause, although stillness is allowed, at the dancers' discretion.

**Procedure**  An accompanist is needed to read aloud. A poem or short prose piece is chosen. The poem, "Mock Orange," by Karen Brodine, who originated the improvisation, is given below. Several Wallace Stevens poems also work well, such as "Anecdote of the Jar," "Autumn Refrain," and "The House Was Quiet and the World Was Calm." Each dancer chooses or is assigned one word that appears in the text, preferably a word that appears more than once.

All the dancers begin at the outer edges of the space, standing or sitting in positions of repose. The accompanist begins to read the text. She should recite the poem slowly and may repeat phrases at her discretion.

When a dancer hears his word he immediately responds by spelling it in movement, using any or all of the methods practiced. He may pause at any time during the spelling. When he has finished, he may remain in the space in his final shape, or take a position of repose either in the space or around the edge. When more than one dancer is in the space, they should relate to the other moving bodies and to the still bodies, considering floor pattern, body design, rhythm, speed, and energy.

If a dancer hears his word again while he is spelling, he should immediately start again at the beginning. Each time a dancer hears his word he should respond immediately with movement.

When the text is finished, dancers complete the words they may be spelling and end in stillness.

### Mock Orange
*by Karen Brodine*

1.
a full length
of words
walking down
the white sheet
thin curtains
cool air
breathing them in

I dreamt the poem
was calm
and complete
something about
petals
white mock orange
cool in darkness

night tag
dash full into
white ghost
mock orange tree's
ripe petals
float past my face
fall on dark grass
bruised, wet with dew.

friends were there
but it was
a lonely poem

serious, full of
round dusk.
what I hold now
is vague scent
of waxy petals
mock scent
mock orange.

2.

up the hill on the sunny side
dip into shadow
touch a cold brick
and stop. wait for that wave
to rush over.
(they call them sleepers)
hot mail box clangs
no letters.
just one cool bill.

now a long afternoon of
hot sun
  cool shower
    warm grass
      iced tea
        cool sheets
          warm forehead
            cold cantaloupe
            warm cat

blank paper
a moth lights
on its glare
as if it's
a lamp
or a flower

I walk into
the mock orange tree
some of its petals
stick to my skin.

# III Time

"However people began to keep time, one imagines the eerie thrill they felt as they found themselves aware of hearing a beat from the outside and of taking a step from the inside, both of them at once. One can still feel a far echo of that thrill as one first finds one's self hitting the beat; or later in life, as one finds one's self stepping securely to a complex rhythm one isn't able to follow consciously" (Edwin Denby, *Dancers, Buildings and People in the Streets*, p. 152). Denby was writing about a primal connection we feel to moving in rhythm. Time is our invisible environment, but we can sense it through a pulse, through rhythm, and by marking off durations of time. This connection we make with rhythm is like a connection to our invisible feelings and a connection of our insides with the outside world.

The improvisations that follow develop rhythmic skill and an awareness of shaping time. Practice and mastery of basic skills lay the groundwork for incorporating rhythm into all of one's movement.

## PULSE

To "take your pulse" is to time your heartbeat. A pulse is a sign of life. It is also a measure of the passing of time. A pulse is the steady beat that underlies our most familiar movements, such as walking and running, and most of the music we hear. It is also a dancer's tool, keeping him "in time" with other dancers.

The following problems introduce pulse through clapping, basic locomotor movements, and free improvisation. Repetitive movement and unison movement are emphasized to ensure a strong connection to the pulse.

### KEEPING A STEADY PULSE: CLAPPING

**Procedure**  The dancers stand in a circle.

One dancer establishes a pulse by clapping. The other dancers join in, clapping in unison. The group should be careful not to speed up or slow down.

The dancer who initiated the pulse stops. Then the others stop. The next person claps a new pulse, and the procedure is repeated.

**Variation**   The dancer who initiates the pulse also introduces a stationary movement to accompany it. This could be swaying the shoulders or hips, alternately clapping high and low or side to side, or stamping.

### KEEPING A STEADY PULSE: TRAVELING

**Procedure**   The dancers stand around the edge of the space.

One dancer enters and walks or runs in the space, keeping a steady pulse with her steps. She may vary her direction of travel: forward, sideways, and backward.

The other dancers join in, walking or running, keeping the pulse constant and in unison. The dancers move anywhere in the space, meeting the eyes of the other dancers as they pass.

The dancer who initiated the traveling exits. The others then exit.

Another person enters, establishing a new pulse, and the procedure is repeated.

### SUBDIVIDING A PULSE

**Preparation**   The dancers are in a circle as large as the space allows. They count off 1,2,1,2 . . . , dividing themselves into two equal groups.

**Procedures**   1. The first group claps a slow, steady pulse initiated by the leader. The second group subdivides the beat into two equal parts by clapping.

The groups reverse roles and repeat.

2. One group claps to establish the pulse, and the other group walks or runs to subdivide it.

The groups reverse roles and repeat.

3. One group claps the pulse. A dancer in the other group uses a repetitive, two-movement sequence to subdivide the pulse. The other dancers in his group join in unison.

The groups reverse roles and repeat.

**Variations**   Repeat these procedures subdividing the pulse into three and then four equal parts. The leader may want to establish a slower pulse for this.

## LOCOMOTOR MOVEMENTS

**Procedure**    Half of the dancers are in the space. Half are around the edge, clapping a moderate pulse.

One of the dancers in the space initiates a repetitive, two-count locomotor step, for example, a side walk, a step-hop, or a step-together. Dancers may volunteer to initiate locomotor steps, or the leader may offer examples. All the dancers in the space do the step in unison.

The groups change roles and repeat, with a new step.

**Variations**    Repeat the procedure with three-count steps, such as skips, gallops, slides, and triplets.

Repeat with four-count steps, which dancers can devise by combining two two-count steps.

**Observation**    The pulse may have to be speeded up or slowed down to suit the various steps.

## FREE MOVEMENT TO A PULSE

**Preparation**    Half of the dancers are in the space. The other half stand around the edge of the space, clapping a moderate pulse. Each dancer in the space has a partner among those clapping.

**Procedures**    1. The dancers in the space move on every pulse. They may walk, move their arms, touch someone, bend, jump, but only on the pulse.

A dancer may leave the center when he chooses. He then joins the clappers, and is replaced in the center by his partner.

2. The clappers sound the pulse. As above, the dancers move on every pulse. They may also subdivide the pulse whenever they choose.

**Observations**    Dancers may find it hard to move only on the pulse, without any subdivisions. When they do subdivide the pulse, is it in a random way, or a repetitive, patterned way?

# ACCENT

A steady beat can mark time. In most Western music, sequences of beats are divided into measures, with the first beat of the measure typically having the accent. The number of beats in a measure is the meter. Within a metered frame-work the following problems explore how accent, suspensions, and pauses give rhythmic shape to regularly metered time.

### ACCENTING RANDOM BEATS

**Procedure**  Everyone stands in a circle as large as the space allows. The leader establishes a fast, steady pulse.

Everyone claps the pulse in unison. At any time a dancer may enter the space and move freely, accenting random beats. The accents should always fall on a beat, never between beats.

When several dancers are in the space together, they relate their movements and the timing of their accents to the movement and accents of the other dancers in the space. Dancers should not clutter the space with too much movement or too great a variety of movement. They may choose to be still while in the center. They may leave when they wish, allowing others to enter.

When a dancer rejoins the outer circle, he resumes clapping the pulse.

After all the dancers have had a few turns to move in the center, they finally all rejoin the circle, to end with everyone clapping the pulse.

**Observations**  The dancers can note whether they tend to accent beats at regular or random intervals, and if they tend to create repetitive patterns of accents. Is this affected by their relating to other dancers in the space? They also may find it hard to avoid accenting movements between the beats.

### MEASURES OF TWO, THREE, FOUR, AND FIVE BEATS

**Procedure**  All the dancers stand in a large circle and clap a steady, moderate pulse initiated by the leader.

One dancer enters the space, regularly accenting the first of every three beats with her movement, thereby establishing a 3/4 meter. The dancer should use the same movement to accent the first beat of every measure. For example, she might stamp a foot or thrust an elbow or hip. Weaker accents may fall anywhere else in the measure, freely improvised.

One at a time, dancers enter the space, moving in the same meter. They use the same movement as was established by the first dancer to accent the first beat of each measure. For the rest of each measure, their movement is freely improvised. Eventually all the dancers are moving and no one is clapping. The basic pulse and measure should be maintained clearly in the movement, even in silence.

Dancers may also choose to be still in the space for part of the time.

Once all the dancers are in the space, they may begin to leave, one at a time, to re-form the circle and resume clapping, being careful to pick up the pulse that is being carried on in the movement.

Eventually all the dancers leave the center and end with everyone clapping the pulse.

**Variations**  Repeat the procedure using 2/4, 4/4, and 5/4 meter. The tempo may be different for each meter.

**Observation**  For most of us it is harder to keep a beat in movement without also hearing it. When there is no sound accompaniment, dancers have to watch each other attentively to keep the pulse steady and in unison.

### CLAPPING METERS I

**Procedure**  The dancers stand in a circle. The leader establishes a moderate tempo, which the dancers keep by stepping in place in unison. A dancer is chosen to be first, with the order proceeding clockwise around the circle.

The first dancer sounds four measures in either 2/4, 3/4, or 4/4 time by clapping the first beat loudly and clapping the other beats softly. The next dancer immediately sounds four measures in one of these meters, without skipping a beat after the end of the last clapper's fourth measure. This procedure continues around the circle.

Inexperienced dancers may want at first to repeat the meter sounded by the previous dancer. Others should choose a new meter.

**Variations**  1. Each dancer sounds only two measures of each meter.

2. In a fast tempo, the dancers sound patterns in four measures and in two measures.

3. The other dancers don't keep the pulse. Each dancer in turn is responsible to keep the continuity of the pulse.

## CLAPPING METERS II: MIXED METERS

**Procedure**  One dancer, by clapping the first beat of each measure loudly and the other beats softly, sounds a two-measure phrase consisting of two different meters (mixed meter). For example, she may clap one measure of 2/4 plus one measure of 3/4. She then repeats these two measures a second time. Together that makes four measures: 2/4 + 3/4 + 2/4 + 3/4. All the dancers immediately repeat these four measures.

The next dancer in turn immediately sounds a new pattern of two different meters, (for example 2/4 plus 4/4), and repeats them once, with the whole group immediately repeating these four measures.

Each repeat of a pattern must follow without losing a beat. Similarly, a new pattern must follow without losing a beat.

Beginners may wish to repeat the same mixed meter as was sounded by the previous clapper. In general, dancers should try to relate their choice of meters to the meters that were just clapped.

**Variations**  1. A dancer may choose to clap either a mixed meter or a repeated meter.

2. Instead of having all the dancers echo the pattern by clapping, only the one who sounded the pattern and the next person in order will clap the pattern a third and fourth time. During these last two repeats, all the other dancers move, accenting their movement on the first beat of each measure, and sustaining movement or moving with weak accents for the rest of the measure. The dancers should finish their movement and resume stepping in place as the next person begins to sound the new pattern.

Dancers should end up in their same places in the circle, so they don't miss their turn as clapper.

## ACCENTS IN COUNTERPOINT

**Preparation**  The dancers count off: one, two, three . . . , until each has a number.

Everyone steps in place, marking out a steady pulse that has been established by the leader. In unison, the odd-numbered dancers clap the first of every three beats, creating measures in 3/4 time. The even-numbered dancers clap the first of every four beats, creating measures of 4/4 time. In this way, everyone should clap the first of every twelve beats in unison.

The pattern of beats looks like this (c = clap, s = step):

```
odds    |c . .|c . .|c . .|c . .|c . .|c . .|c . .|c . .|
all      s s s s s s s s s s s s|s s s s s s s s s s s s|
evens   |c . . .|c . . .|c . . .|c . . .|c . . .|c . . .|
```

Repeat, with the odds clapping 4/4 meter and the evens clapping 3/4 meter.

**Procedure**   The dancers are at one end of the space. They pair up in order: one with two, three with four, and so on. The odds step and clap 3/4 meter. The evens step and clap 4/4 meter, as above.

At a cue from the leader, the first duet begins. The two dancers move across the space, each one accenting in movement the first beat of every measure in his own meter. (The duet need no longer clap.) Additional, weaker accents may be freely improvised.

Dancers should maintain their own meter clearly. Each one should also try to be aware of his partner's contrasting meter.

After twenty-four beats, the next two dancers begin to move across the space.

When the dancers arrive across the space, they resume stepping and clapping.

All dancers should have a turn to go across the floor at least once in each meter.

**Variations**   1. The odds are on one side of the space and the evens are on the other side. They clap only the accents without stepping time between. If an even dancer enters the space, an odd dancer must join to make a duet, and vice versa. One or more such pairs enter the space and perform duets, accenting in counterpoint as before and traveling anywhere in the space. They may leave when they wish and rejoin their group of clappers. Additional duets may enter the space at any time.

2. The accompanists mark time in place, but clap only the first of every twelve beats. Duets enter and leave when they wish. The dancers must keep track of their own accents.

3. Duets move across the space in 3/4 and 5/4 time, with accompanists. Each new duet begins after thirty beats.

4. Try variation 3 with music in 4/4 time, so that both dancers are moving against the meter of the music.

**Observation**    Some of the variations are difficult and may be appropriate only for more advanced dancers.

### MIXED METER: COUNTERPOINT

**Preparation**    In Clapping Meters II: Mixed Meters, the dancers practiced adding meters, creating phrases of mixed meter. They've also moved with their Accents in Counterpoint. With this background, the dancers may familiarize themselves with some of the more complex meters to be found in musical composition and in the folk music and dance of other nationalities: 5/4, 6/8, 7/8, and 9/8. These meters usually include secondary accents within the measure. Here are some familiar patterns of accents for these meters:

| | | |
|---|---|---|
| 5/4 = 3/4 + 2/4 | or | 2/4 + 3/4 |
| 6/8 = 3/8 + 3/8 | or | 2/8 + 2/8 + 2/8 |
| 7/8 = 3/8 + 2/8 + 2/8 | or | 2/8 + 2/8 + 3/8 |
| 9/8 = 3/8 + 3/8 + 3/8 | or | 3/8 + 2/8 + 2/8 + 2/8 |

To familiarize themselves with these rhythmic patterns, the dancers stand in a circle, sounding the patterns by clapping each major and minor accent loudly and all the other beats softly. In addition, dancers may say "One" on the major accent that begins each measure.

Once the dancers have sounded out each rhythmic pattern in unison, they should divide into two groups. Each group sounds one of the two given variations of a chosen meter, so that the main accent is sounded in unison, and the minor accents fall in counterpoint to each other. Dancers should establish their own rhythm clearly, and should listen to the accents of the other group as well.

**Procedure**    All the dancers stand around the outside of the space. The leader chooses one of these meters: 5/4, 6/8, 7/8, or 9/8. Half of the group sounds one rhythm in this meter, while the other half sounds the other rhythm, as practiced in the preparation.

At their discretion, dancers may stop sounding the rhythm and move into the space, accenting the rhythm with their movements. They should be aware of the accents of the other dancers' movements.

Dancers may leave the space and become accompanists when they choose.

This may be repeated with each of the four meters listed above.

**Observation**    If the dancers have difficulty in moving to these patterns of accents, they can practice together first with steps to the beat, stepping low on the accents, and high on the rest of the beats.

### OMITTED BEATS

**Procedures**    All the dancers are in the space. The leader claps or provides music with a clear 4/4 meter.

1. The dancers move percussively on every beat and are still between the beats.

2. The dancers accent every beat and sustain their movement between beats.

3. Omitting the second beat in every measure, the dancers move percussively on the first, third, and fourth beats, and are still between accents.

4. Omitting the third beat of every measure, dancers accent the first, second, and fourth beats, and sustain their movement between accents. Movement is sustained through the omitted beat.

5. Omitting the fourth beat of every measure, dancers accent the first three beats, using percussive and sustained movements at their discretion.

6. The dancers omit one beat in each measure. It need not be the same beat each time. They may use percussive and sustained movements, as they choose.

### SYNCOPATION

Syncopation is the displacement of the regular metrical accent to a weak beat or to between beats.

**Procedures**    All the dancers are in the space. The leader claps a steady 4/4 meter or provides music with a clear 4/4 meter.

1. Dancers move on every "and" beat (the upbeat) and sustain their movement or stay still between their accents.

2. Dancers may accent any beat or "and" beat, except for the first beat in each measure. They may use both percussive and sustained movement, as they choose.

## INDIVIDUAL RHYTHMIC ACCENTS

**Procedure**   A moderate pulse is established by music, clapping, or a metronome.

All the dancers move individually in the space, using steps and movement impulses in the torso to accent their movements.

As dancers become comfortable with creating accents, they explore rhythmic variations: sometimes accenting the beat, sometimes omitting the beat, sometimes accenting the "and" beat. More experienced dancers may also accent other internal subdivisions of the beat.

Movement may be percussive or sustained. Stillness is allowed. Dancers should move fully and should never lose their performance presence, whether moving or still.

## EIGHT-COUNT RHYTHMIC PHRASES

**Preparation**   The leader establishes a steady pulse, with clapping or a metronome. Each dancer sets an eight-count phrase containing five accents, not all of which fall on a beat. The phrase should travel, so that four repetitions of the phrase take the dancer across the space. The phrase should include some percussive movement and some sustained movement.

**Procedure**   The dancers stand in pairs at one end of the space and clap the same pulse as in the preparation, with the first of every eight beats a strong beat.

One pair at a time moves across the space, with each dancer performing his own phrase, being aware of his accents in relation to his partner's accents.

After everyone has had a turn, repeat this with different partners.

**Observations**   Some pairs will complement each other especially well. This may be because of their rhythmic relationships, levels, or the shape and direction of the movement. The dancers can identify these duets and repeat them for the group to see.

## GROUP RHYTHMIC ACCENTS

**Preparation**   The dancers gather into groups of three or four. Each group sets a short phrase which includes both percussive and sustained movements.

The precise rhythm of this phrase need not be set.

**Procedure**   If there are only a few small groups, one group dances while the others watch. Otherwise, more than one group may dance at a time.

Members of the audience keep the pulse by clapping, snapping fingers, or making mouth sounds.

Each small group improvises together on its theme, using both percussive and sustained movements. Repetition of parts of the phrase is allowed. Dancers should relate their accents, suspensions, and moments of stillness to those of the other dancers.

# METRICAL RHYTHM

The characteristics of Latin music are distinct from rock music; ragtime music is distinct from classical music. Most people know a cha cha from a mambo; some even know a gigue from a gavotte. That recognition lies primarily in their sense of the different rhythms. When dancing, people connect to the rhythm of the music.

In its own right, dance can create strong rhythms, which can be used to establish relationships among the dancers. This section offers ways to unite the dancers' ability to hear rhythms with their physical rhythmic sense.

### CLAPPING RHYTHMS

**Procedure**   Everyone stands in a circle. One person begins by clapping either a moderate pulse or a simple rhythm within a four-beat measure (such as 1 + 2   3   4 +), sounding a strong accent on the first beat. This is the base rhythm.

Others join in at their discretion, clapping rhythmic patterns in the same meter. Each person should repeat his pattern consistently. These rhythms need not have a strong downbeat. Anyone may stop clapping at any time, continue to listen, and rejoin with a new rhythm. To avoid a thick or muddy sound, dancers can clap sparse rhythms or spend more time listening without clapping.

**Variations**   1. Repeat, including other means of sound production: slapping, snapping, vocal and mouth sounds.

2. Repeat, using measures of three, five, or six beats, depending on the level of the group.

**Observations**    For some, it may take several measures of clapping to get a rhythm clearly established. Once it is set, it should remain consistent.

If the reliable base rhythm is discontinued, some clappers may have difficulty keeping track of the meter. In this case, either they or someone else can establish a new base rhythm.

### REPRODUCING RHYTHMS

**Procedure**    Everyone stands in a circle. One person is designated to start. The order will proceed clockwise around the circle. The leader establishes a steady 4/4 meter.

The first person claps a one-measure rhythmic pattern in 4/4 meter, and then repeats it once, without losing a beat. The group immediately repeats the pattern twice. Keeping the continuity of the pulse and meter, the second person then claps a one-measure pattern twice, which the group immediately repeats twice. This continues around the circle, until everyone has initiated a rhythmic pattern.

**Variations**    1. Repeat using other sounds.
2. Repeat using other meters.
3. Dancers may either sound the rhythm or move to that rhythm in response to each new pattern.

**Observations**    If the group has difficulty in sustaining the pulse or meter, the leader may clap the meter, accenting the first beat, while the dancers clap their rhythms over this. Beginners may clap very simple rhythms, or may repeat or slightly vary the preceding rhythm.

### WALKING RHYTHMS

**Procedure**    The leader claps a moderate pulse to which pairs of dancers walk in the space. For simplicity they may walk in a large circle.

While one dancer in each pair continues to walk at a steady pace, the other dancer makes a rhythmic pattern of steps and hops that travels alongside his partner. The pattern may be done in any meter, but should be repeated a number of times until it is clearly established and consistent. The dancer may then resume walking at a steady pace in unison with his partner. Now the partner may change to a rhythmic pattern of steps.

The dancers repeat this several times. Then each pair may show a few rhythms to the rest of the group.

**Variation**  More advanced dancers may do this in trios, with two of the three dancers traveling with rhythmic patterns while one walks to the pulse. The patterns should relate to each other.

**Observations**  If the rhythmic pattern of steps travels more or less than simple walking, the person walking may be able to adjust the length of her stride to stay alongside her partner, or the person with the pattern can zigzag or travel backward as well as forward.

If beginners have trouble making a pattern, they can walk double time or skip to the pulse, or try any simple, repeatable step.

### RHYTHMIC MOVEMENT: TRIOS

**Procedure**  The group is divided into trios. One trio at a time will move, with the rest of the dancers as accompanists. The leader establishes a 4/4 meter, which the accompanists sound by clapping on the first beat and clicking or snapping on the other three beats of each measure.

The trio begins off the space. One dancer enters and performs a movement phrase of one measure. The dancer repeats this phrase, keeping the rhythm consistent, though she may do variations on the movement motif. The accents and suspensions within the phrase should be clearly visible.

The second dancer enters as soon as possible, with a phrase that relates to the original, both in rhythm and movement. He repeats this phrase, keeping the rhythm consistent, allowing some variation in the movement.

The third dancer enters as soon as possible, with a phrase that relates to the other two phrases, both in rhythm and movement. She repeats this phrase, keeping the rhythm consistent, allowing some variation in the movement.

These trios should be brief. Once the trio is clearly established, one dancer may end in stillness. The others then end in stillness, with attention to the static design of the ending.

**Variations**    1. Repeat with other meters.

2. Repeat without any sound accompaniment. The trio should keep their measures synchronized.

3. Repeat with two-measure phrases.


### RHYTHMIC ACCOMPANIMENT

**Procedure**    The group is divided into pairs. One member of each pair will begin as a dancer and the other as an accompanist. Everyone starts around the edge of the space.

One dancer enters and moves, establishing a phrase of movement with a consistent rhythmic pattern in 3/4 meter. The movement may vary somewhat from repetition to repetition, but the rhythm should remain consistent.

As soon as he can, the partner of the dancer makes a sound accompaniment that exactly reproduces the rhythm of the movement phrase. He may use any means of sound production available. Once established, the accompaniment should not vary either in rhythm or in means of sound production as long as the dancing partner is in the space.

One at a time, other dancers enter the space, basing their movement on that of the original dancer, although some variation is welcome. The accompanists will reproduce their rhythms in sound. The rhythm of each additional dancer should relate to the rhythms already established.

At any time, a dancer may leave the space and exchange roles with his partner, becoming an accompanist, while the partner becomes a dancer.

The roles may change back and forth several times before the problem ends.

**Observations**    The original phrase of movement will greatly affect the ability to make clear rhythmic phrases. The dancers may have made observations in the last problem, Rhythmic Movement: Trios, that help them make an appropriate original phrase for this problem. In some cases, if an original phrase presents difficulties, the leader may choose to interrupt and ask the dancers to start again.

### RHYTHMIC COUNTERPOINT: A ROUND

**Preparation**    Three rhythmic lines are given below. Each one is a measure in 3/4 meter.

| Musical Notation | Counts |
|---|---|
| ♩ ♩ ♩ | 1   2   3 |
| ♫ ♩ ♫ | 1 + 2    3 + a |
| ♩. ♪♫ | 1    +    + |

The dancers practice each line separately, first by clapping the pattern of accents, then by moving with these accents.

Dividing into three groups, the dancers now clap the pattern as a round, with the leader conducting and cuing the entrances. The first group begins. The second group waits three counts before beginning, and the third group waits three more counts before beginning. Each group will clap the three-line rhythmic pattern from the beginning and repeat it without pause until the leader cues an end.

**Procedure**    One member of each group will be a dancer, while the others accompany.

Each group of accompanists should have its own means of producing sound: claps, snaps, wood blocks, drums, voice, and so forth, which is different from any other group's. The accompanists begin as above, with the leader cuing them to begin. After two rounds of the pattern, the dancers begin to move in rhythm with their accompanists, accenting the sounded accents, and sustaining their movement or being still between the accents. The movement and spacing may vary, in response to the other dancers, but the rhythmic counterpoint should be visible.

At any time an accompanist may enter and join the movement. This is a cue for the dancer in her group then in the space to leave and join the accompanists.

**Variation**    Repeat with no other accompaniment than clapping a steady pulse with accents on the first beat of each measure. The dancers are responsible to keep the pattern of accents.

**Observation**    The more a dancer can evolve a consistent sequence of movement, the less difficult it should be to relate to the other two dancers and maintain rhythmic accuracy.

### CANON

**Procedure**    The dancers arrange themselves in single files of three or four dancers each. The dancer at the front of each line will be a leader. Music or clapping establishes a moderate pulse in 4/4 time. The leader moves continuously, in relation to the music. The second in line observes what the leader is doing and imitates as precisely as possible, but four beats later. The third person watches the second person and imitates four beats later, and so forth. In this way the dancers will be moving in canon.

The leader should always face away from his followers, since, if he faces them, they have to turn away from him and can no longer see to imitate.

**Observations**    This problem can be quite challenging, since it requires that dancers learn one series of movements while they execute another. To make the problem easier, leaders can perform movements that start at the beginning of the measure and last four counts.

For a less strict version of the canon, see Loose Canon in the section on Nonmetrical Rhythms.

## NONMETRICAL RHYTHMS

Rhythm is inherent in all movement: ocean waves, the flight of birds, the lurching of heavy machinery. Many of these rhythms, especially the natural ones, are not based on a regular pulse. Even someone's ordinarily steady walk will speed up to cross a street and slow down in front of a shop window or a sunset. Emotions exhibit their own rhythms, such as jerky nervousness or bounding gaiety. People are aware of these rhythms in each other's movements, even if not consciously, and respond to them; they tend to imitate each other's rhythms when they feel in harmony and resist them in conflict.

Not all dance movement is based on a metrical pulse. Some movements have their own inherent rhythms which, when chained together with other movements, create nonmetrical phrases. Even when set to metrical music, movement may go across the beats, relating only broadly to the musical phrasing. A "rhythmic" dancer has a sense of the rhythms inherent in the movement and an ability to relate these to the framework of a musical accompaniment.

## COUNTING NUMBERS

**Procedure**  Everyone sits in a circle. The dancers will count out loud in order, 1,2,3 . . . , going around the circle, with each dancer saying one number. Dancers will give rhythmic shape to the sound, so that it is prolonged, staccato, stuttered, hissed, and so forth. There should be variety in the volume and voice quality, as well as in the timing between numbers.

Once every dancer has said a number, they repeat this sequence from memory. (They shouldn't be warned beforehand.)

**Variations**  1. The dancers repeat the procedure, adding movement to the sound, and then reproduce this sequence from memory.

2. The dancers count around the circle, saying any number they choose. Numbers may be repeated. Sounds may overlap. The dancers can give form to the overall phrasing by the recurrent use of certain numbers and sounds.

3. The dancers repeat variation 2, including movement with the sound. They should still be attentive to the overall phrasing, rather than to individual inventiveness.

**Observations**  The accompanying sound gives an additional sense of the phrasing of the movement. Were the dancers more accurate in repeating sounds or movement?

## NONMETRIC PHRASE SEQUENCES

**Procedure**  The dancers sit in a circle. Using breath sounds, vocalized sounds, clucking, whistling, clapping, snapping, stamping, and so on, each dancer in turn makes a short, nonmetric rhythmic pattern of sound. Succeeding phrases should grow out of preceding ones.

**Variations**  1. Phrases may overlap, so that a new phrase begins before the preceding one or more have finished.

2. Dancers add movement to the sounds.

## NONMETRIC SOUND AND MOVEMENT

**Procedure**  The dancers start off the space. One dancer enters, moving with attention to the phrasing of her movement, and creating sound that parallels the movement phrasing. At any time, another dancer may enter the space, relating his movement design and dynamic phrasing to that of the first dancer. Dancers may enter and leave when they wish. There should not, however, be so many dancers in the space that the phrasing relationships become cluttered or blurred.

Dancers may explore a variety of movement dynamics: sustained, staccato, suspended, heavy, vibratory, swinging, gliding.

**Variation**   Repeat, without using sound.

**Observation**   For some, the sound assists their perception of the phrasing; for others, it inhibits their movement.

### SINGLE MOVEMENTS

**Procedures**   1. The dancers are scattered throughout the space. They individually explore physical means to initiate movement. These may include: impulses in part of the body, giving in to gravity, breathing, and shifts of weight. Each motivation will engender some movement: a turn, a step, a suspension, a fall, a shudder, a twist. Some movements will be very brief, some longer. Each will have some sort of ending: a fade, a sudden stop, or a follow-through. Dancers should explore the endings of movements, sometimes finding their own spontaneous sense of fulfilling the movement, sometimes cutting it short, and sometimes extending it as much as they can, still feeling that the movement is a continuation of the original motivation.

Dancers then show each other a variety of single movements.

2. Each dancer chains together a sequence of several movements, creating a rhythmic phrase. This can be done in various ways: continuously, not interrupting the flow of the movement; with sudden changes; subsiding and reviving; and so forth. Individual movements in these sequences should be of various lengths.

Dancers show each other their phrases.

**Observations**   Do some dancers tend toward a consistent type of rhythmic pattern in their sequences? They can repeat the problem, trying to find other rhythmic shapes for their phrases.

### PHRASE LENGTHS

**Procedure**  Seven dancers stand together in a close group. They are assigned an order, from one to seven. (This may also be done with fewer or more dancers.)

The dancers should keep in mind the ways they initiated and ended movement in the last problem, Single Movements.

Dancer number one does a single movement and is still. Immediately, dancer two does a two-movement phrase and is still. Dancer three does a three-movement phrase and is still. This continues until dancer number seven does a seven-movement phrase, after which all seven dancers immediately do seven-movement phrases at the same time. Immediately, dancer number one does a seven-movement phrase, number two does a six-movement phrase, number three does a five-movement phrase, until dancer number seven does one movement. Immediately all do one movement and are still.

The moving dancer should relate to the others spatially. Dancers should end in stillness in positions that allow them to see the rest of the group. Since single movements can vary in length, there will be some difficulty in keeping track of the number of movements done by the others. Dancers should judge as best they can and proceed at their own discretion.

### BREATH PHRASES

**Procedures**  1. *Vibrations.* All the dancers lie on their backs. Breathing easily and regularly, they gradually let the exhalation produce a sound. By varying the pitch, they can feel vibrations in different parts of the body. The head and chest are easiest to feel. Can they feel the vibrations elsewhere as well?

2. *Rising and sinking.* The leader names parts of the body: chest, right arm, shoulders, hips, knees, left foot, and so on. When a body part is named, the dancers lift that part off the floor as they inhale and ease it back down when they exhale.

3. *Wavelike movement.* Motivated by breathing, and using any parts of the body in any sequence, the dancers create wavelike movements in their bodies. They should use this to bring themselves gradually to standing.

4. *Breath phrases.* The dancers explore movements that arise from their

breathing. They may try expanding movements such as opening the torso and arms as they inhale and sinking or subsiding movements as they exhale. Or they may try more vigorous movements such as swings on the exhale and suspensions on the inhale. Gradually, the dancers should put together sequences of these movements, considering the rhythmic and dynamic shape of their phrases.

After a while, dancers may begin to imitate and vary each other's movements. They may join into duets and trios briefly, then circulate and interact with other dancers.

## LOOSE CANON

**Procedure**   Half the dancers are audience. Half are in the space, arranged in groups of three. One dancer in each group is the leader. Keeping their backs to their followers, the leaders move with an awareness of the rhythms created in their movement. Followers imitate their leaders in a loose canon, sometimes moving at the same speed, but several counts behind, sometimes slowing down part of the movement, then speeding up or eliminating some of the movement to catch up. The followers should create a rhythmic interaction with their leader and each other.

Each dancer should have a turn as leader.

**Observations**   Followers can perceive how the rhythms in the leader's movement generate rhythmic possibilities for the followers. This should make them more effective when their turn comes as leader.

For work in strict canonical form, see Canon in the section on Metrical Rhythm.

## RHYTHMIC VARIATIONS

**Procedure**   The dancers begin off the space. One dancer enters and introduces a movement motif which the group will use as the basis for variations. One at a time dancers enter and move in ways that develop the material introduced by the first dancer. The dancers should relate to each other rhythmically, echoing and playing off each other's phrasing and accents. Not too many dancers should be in the space at the same time, so that they can be aware of each other. Dancers may enter and leave at any time.

When it seems that the first theme has been well explored, another dancer may enter and introduce a new theme, which the dancers will develop through variations. No more than two themes should be going on at the same time.

This improvisation can go on for any length of time. The dancers should keep it going for as long as they feel they are rhythmically interesting.

**Observations**    Attention to the rhythm should ideally be present in all of the dancers' movement. Other improvisations that give the dancers the opportunity to develop their rhythmic awareness are Walking, Running, and Stillness in Groupings; Moving a Series of Shapes and the variation on Waves of Movement in Shape and Shape Sequences; Dynamic Variations in Dynamics; and most of the problems in Theme and Variations.

## DURATION AND SPEED

How long is long? The Entrance of the Shades in *La Bayadère* continues for several minutes, while a long train of dancers repeats an adagio arabesque and port de bras. Sufi dancers spin for hours at a time. If in five minutes one dance packs in a great amount of movement and another presents a few slow phrases, are both dances the same length? How much does movement alter our perspective on time?

### ESTIMATING DURATION

**Procedures**    1. The leader has a watch, clock, or stopwatch for counting seconds. Each dancer will have a turn at estimating a given span of time, measured in seconds.

The leader designates whose turn it is, the length of time to be estimated (varying from dancer to dancer, ranging from five seconds to thirty seconds), and when the time begins.

The dancer indicates when he thinks the time is up. The leader then tells what the dancer's estimated time actually was. All the other dancers can be trying to estimate at the same time.

2. The dancer starts moving at the cue for the time to begin and freezes when he thinks the time is up.

3. Repeat, moving fast.

4. Repeat, moving slowly.

**Observations**    Do the dancers generally over- or underestimate the durations? Is this equally the case for five-second and thirty-second durations? Do the dancers count silently to keep track of the time? This is harder to do while moving. What happens then? What sorts of movement do they tend to do? Why? How does the speed of the movement affect accuracy in timing?

### REPETITION AND DURATION

**Procedure**    Dancers begin off the space. One dancer enters and performs a repetitive movement or phrase of movement. At any time, a dancer may enter and perform her own repetitive movement or phrase. The movement may be stationary or may travel through space.

    The dancers should decide how long to continue their movement before leaving the space. This should depend on what else is going on at the same time, and for how long it has continued. Some dancers may stay on for a long time, while others may make quick appearances which highlight the more enduring phrases.

**Observations**    When a movement continues for a long time one's perception of it changes. It can take on more value or become tedious. There may not be consensus as to when this happens. It will, however, most likely depend on what else is going on at the same time.

### 8 7 6 5 4 3 2 1

**Preparation**    Each dancer stands at a spot A that he's chosen, being sure to identify its location. Each dancer then chooses another spot B and stands there, and identifies this location. Each dancer should walk to A and then back to B to become comfortable with locating these spots.

**Procedure**    Depending on the size of the space, a group of six to ten dancers is in the space. Each dancer stands at his spot A.

    The leader provides an accompaniment of slow eights, either with music or by counting.

    At the leader's cue, the dancers travel however they wish, each from his A to his B, taking the full eight counts to arrive. They immediately return to A, taking seven counts to arrive and holding perfectly still on count eight. Then they return to B in six counts, and hold still counts

87654321. **Making an all-out effort to cross the space in that one final count.**

seven and eight. They continue this way until they must travel from B to A on one count, and then hold counts two through eight.

For most dancers, the last one or two attempts to reach their spot on time will not succeed.

My friend Moss liked this problem because he never thought that something's being impossible should get in the way of doing it.

### FAST, MEDIUM, AND SLOW

**Preparations**     1. The dancers are scattered throughout the space. Without traveling, the dancers will move fast, medium, or slow, in response to instructions from the leader.

2. The dancers practice getting across the space quickly, then in a moderate time, then taking a long time.

**Procedure**     A group of three to eight dancers moves across the space in accordance with two instructions: whether to use fast, medium, or slow movement, and the number of seconds it will take to get across. Dancers should move in a generally direct path at an even rate of travel.

The leader should vary the instructions for each group, and each group should have a chance to try several variations of speed and duration.

At first, the leader may count the seconds. Later, the dancers may estimate the duration as best they can as they move.

**Observation**    The dancers may find it difficult to coordinate slow movement with rapid travel, and fast movement with slow travel, or to keep track of the duration without counts. Practice will help.

## ACCELERATION AND DECELERATION

**Preparations**    1. All the dancers pace slowly across the space while the leader times how long it takes to go from one end of the space to the other.

2. In the same length of time it takes for the dancers to pace slowly across the space, they proceed at a steady rate of travel, beginning with very fast movement and gradually decelerating to very slow movement, reaching medium speed about half way across the space.

3. Repeat this, accelerating from very slow movement to very fast.

**Procedure**    In the same time period used in the preparation, trios travel across the space. One of the dancers paces across slowly, acting as a space marker for the others. The second dancer crosses the space, decelerating from fast to slow movement. The third dancer crosses the space, accelerating from slow to fast movement. All three should keep generally abreast as they proceed. If possible, the second and third dancers can relate their movements to each other.

All speed changes should be gradual. Dancers should have turns at each of the three roles.

**Variation**    Try duets, without anyone to pace out the space.

## SUDDEN CHANGES OF SPEED

**Preparation**    The dancers should review Following in Unison, with attention to keeping continuity of the movement when passing the leadership from one dancer to another.

**Procedure**    Half the dancers watch. Half the dancers follow in unison.

When a dancer is leading the group, she may at any time suddenly change the speed of her movement. Leaders should, however, be fairly repetitive in their movement, especially in their fast movement, so that the other dancers can follow. The dancers should follow as best they can, never losing performance presence, even when movement is fast or when the leadership changes.

When the leadership changes, the new leader should keep the current speed of movement at least briefly before changing, so that the transitions between leaders have continuity.

**Variation**    Rather than having the dancer who is leading decide on the speed changes, the members of the audience call out the changes: fast, medium, or slow.

### CONTRASTS

**Procedure**    Small groups of three to five dancers take turns in the space doing improvisations based on two related but contrasting instructions utilizing elements of time. Examples are stop and go, slow and fast, lengthy and brief.

**Variation**    A group decides on a contrasting pair of instructions, without divulging what it is. The audience can guess.

### VARIATIONS ON SPEED

**Preparation**    The dancers divide into groups of four or five. Each group will put together a thematic phrase consisting of travel, turn, drop, reach, in any order. There should be little or no repetition in the thematic phrase.

**Procedure**    One group at a time is in the space. Their movement is limited to the thematic phrase, repetitions of parts of the phrase, and speed changes, both gradual and sudden. Dancers should use unison, canon, and repetition to relate to each other.

# IV Movement Invention

Group improvisations unite structure and invention. To complement the structuring elements of time and space, a section on movement invention focuses on imagination. From mimetic devices, such as characterization, to abstract devices, such as theme and variation, these improvisations represent approaches to finding new movement.

## IMAGES

Imagery, by directing the dancer toward new ways of moving, represents a fertile source of movement for the dancer who is interested in abstraction as well as for the one who wants his movement to be more literally evocative.

The images presented in this section can address the dancers' movement limitations. Ballet-trained dancers may profit from exploring the use of weight and use of the torso. They might work with images of stones, clay, or rippling water. Perpetually active dancers might try being rocks or lizards.

Other sections of this book also work with images. In the section on Dynamics, improvisations using imagery help extend the dancers' dynamic range. In the section on Props, concrete objects are the image source.

Most of the problems in this section are focused more on movement exploration than on developing the movement through group structures. For further development, imagery exploration can be alternated with some of the walking dance problems in the chapter on Space. Then the two can be combined, joining defined spatial structures with the movement generated through imagery. The images in this section can also be developed by methods used in the section on Levels of Abstraction.

### ENVIRONMENTS

**Procedure**  The leader names an environment from the following list. First the dancers all move in the space at the same time, interacting as seems appropriate to them. Then they should have the chance to observe the different solutions that various dancers found.

Walk against a wind.
Walk through a storm.
Walk uphill. Return downhill.
Walk in mud.
Walk over a log bridge.
Feel the heat. Feel the cold.
Pass through trees and brush.

### QUICK IMAGES

**Procedure**    The dancers begin off the space. The leader names an image. Any number of dancers may enter, responding quickly and briefly with movement or a static design to produce an immediate visual image. A list of possible images follows.

| | |
|---|---|
| people at the beach | noise |
| the beach | quiet |
| Canada geese | rain |
| a wheat field | snow |
| an assembly line | a crowd |

**Observation**    The emphasis in this problem should be on finding an immediate visual image, not on developing a scene. Otherwise, this problem can turn out to be a vehicle for platitudes and play-acting.

### ANIMALS

**Procedure**    The leader names an animal from the list. All the dancers move as the named animal.

| | | |
|---|---|---|
| cat | snake | hawk |
| lion | lizard | monkey |
| chicken | frog | butterfly |
| beetle | dog | fish |
| bee | kangaroo | ape |
| deer | horse | woodpecker |
| spider | | |

**Quick Images: Noise**

**Variation**   Dancers may also interact as different animals, for instance, a cat with a dog.

**Observations**   This problem is effective in getting dancers with set movement habits to move in ways unfamiliar to them. It can be used as a starting point for helping dancers be aware of their tendencies.

I saw a student of mine transformed during this improvisation. As a human, he had a particularly stylized and limited way of moving; but he moved magnificently as a leopard and as a snake.

### LAUGH, GIGGLE, SOB

**Procedure**   The leader names an action from the list below. The dancers may begin by producing the action as literally as possible. They may then begin to abstract it by using other parts of the body, clarifying the rhythmic pattern or exaggerating the movement in some way. Dancers may suggest other actions.

| | | |
|---|---|---|
| laugh | giggle | sob |
| whimper | cough | sneeze |
| choke | tickle | itch |
| shiver | | |

### SIMPLE MOVEMENT VIGNETTES

**Procedure**   Small groups of three to five dancers take turns in the space doing one-minute improvisations in response to an instruction. Examples of instructions include: round, fast, sudden, elongated, together. The same instruction may be used for more than one group.

**Variation**   Without deciding on an instruction, a small group begins off the space. One of the dancers is asked to start. This dancer enters with a specific idea in mind and moves accordingly. All the dancers in the small group should enter, move in accordance with what they perceive their leader to have established, and find an ending after about a minute.

### NARRATIVES

**Procedure**   The leader names a sequence of actions that can form a narrative, based on human or nonhuman activity. Depending on which seems appropriate to the actions named, the dancers may work as a group or as individuals.

A drought, a stream, a flood.
Water in a pot, boiling, evaporating.
Alone, together, lonely.
The preparation, the trip, the fatigue.
Morning, noon, and night.
Fire and water make smoke.
Thunder, lightning, rain.

The dancers should shape their improvisations with a clear beginning, middle, and end.

### CLICHÉS

**Procedure**  Clichés are not the enemies of inventiveness. If taken literally, many cli-chés and often-used expressions produce surprising movement images. A long list of such expressions follows.

Each dancer chooses a cliché and decides on a way to structure it into an improvisation for one or more dancers. The structure should be simple, so that it can be explained quickly to the group that will be danc-ing. To save time, two or more groups can be learning their instructions at once.

One group at a time enters the space and performs. If they don't tell which cliché was the basis for their improvisation, the audience can guess.

**Clichés: Over One's Head. Each dancer had to have a part of his own body, or someone else's, over his head at all times.**

| | |
|---|---|
| armed to the teeth | at loose ends |
| at one fell swoop | bow and scrape |
| by leaps and bounds | done to a turn |
| down and out | down at heel and out at elbow |
| draw the line | fall head over heels |
| far-reaching effects | fast and furious |
| finishing touch | firm footing |
| follow in someone's footsteps | from head to foot, top to toe |
| hanging in the balance | hard and fast |
| hold one's own | have no leg to stand on |
| in full swing | in good hands |
| in the long run | lose one's grip |
| make ends meet | neither here nor there |
| on someone's right side | on the spot |
| over and above | over one's head |
| play fast and loose | pull one's weight |
| push comes to shove | put one's foot down |
| put one's best foot forward | stand or fall |
| straight and narrow | straight from the shoulder |
| take immediate steps | take it or leave it |
| take the wrong turn | take to one's heels |
| the long and the short of it | throw someone over |
| touch and go | toe the line |
| turn one's back | up in arms |
| ups and downs | wait on someone hand and foot |

**Observation**    If time is short, the dancers can take a list of clichés home and devise their structures for the next meeting. This is a simple way to initiate the dancers into devising improvisations themselves.

## LEVELS OF ABSTRACTION

Periodically through the history of dance the question whether dance should be pure form or whether it should imitate life has flared into a full-blown controversy. In practice, dance has seemed to alternate between periods that emphasize expression or emphasize form. Of course, this distinction is not absolute. All dance, whether abstract or mimetic, is supported by a well-formed struc-

**Clichés: Making Ends Meet**

ture. No dance, whether mimetic or abstract, can escape the expressiveness of human movement.

Using familiar gestures and movements as its source, this section explores the effects of abstracting movement. It gives dancers and actors the chance to examine the effects of form on literal movement and the presence of expression in abstract movement. They have the chance to practice making the distinction between the literal and abstract in their own movement.

For choreographers, this section offers an inexhaustible source of dance movement through the stylization and abstraction of ordinary gestures.

## HAND GESTURES

**Procedures** This problem is an adaptation of Hand Dialogues in Shape and Shape Sequences, focusing on making the distinction between gestural movement and abstract movement.

1. Pairs of dancers face each other. One dancer makes a gesture with her hand or hands whose meaning can be recognized by the partner:

thumbs up, a fist, the peace sign, the victory sign, pointing, palm forward for stop, palm up for begging, and so forth. The partner then makes a hand gesture in response. The first person responds to her partner, and the exchange continues. Dancers may use one or both hands. They should hold each gesture until the partner has responded, then make a new gesture. This will be a series of still positions, rather than a sequence of movements.

The dancers should develop a human interaction through these gestures. It could be threat and retreat, courtship, camaraderie, giving directions. Once the pairs have done this for a while, each pair can show an excerpt of its exchange to the others.

2. Repeating the same procedure, the pairs now carry on hand dialogues that do not have a literal relationship, but an abstract one. As before, each dancer makes a gesture in response to his partner. Some of the same gestures may appear, like thumbs up, but the partner should respond to the shape and placement of the hands, rather than to what the gesture implies. Pairs should try to develop one motif for a while before going on to another. There should be as much coherence in the abstract sequences as in the gestural sequences, although the coherence will depend on formal, rather than dramatic, relationships.

**Variation**    Repeat both procedures allowing continuous movement of the hands as well as still positions. Both dancers can be "talking" at once, as long as they don't allow their dialogue to degenerate into chaos.

## DRAMATIC INTENTIONS

**Procedures**    1. The dancers divide into small groups of about three dancers each. Each group will decide on a dramatic intention. They may choose their own, or pick one from the following list: hide, hit, dodge, forget, get free, be seen, get comfortable, remember, stay upright. Groups may first want to work all at once, without an audience. Each group should find movement that expresses the chosen intention. After exploring its topic for a while, one group at a time can improvise for the rest of the dancers. The movement may be performed literally or in a more dramatically stylized way, whichever seems appropriate to the topic. For example, dancers may not want to hit each other literally; they may be happy to get comfortable literally.

2. The groups use the movements arising from these motivations as a basis for abstraction. They should consider the formal components of movement: shape, spatial relationships, rhythm, and dynamics. The dancers should use some of these elements as they appeared in their original movement, but should change others. (Someone might choose to punch lazily, in an upward direction, or with a hip.) In this way they can generate a range of movements and group relationships that are of interest without being dramatic or literal.

**Observations**  This exercise gives dancers practice in distinguishing between various levels of abstraction. It also offers a good method for generating both abstract movement and movement that retains recognizable dramatic motivations.

### TABLEAUX

**Procedures**  Half the dancers are in the space. The other half are audience. The group in the space chooses a situation and creates a tableau that suggests the chosen situation. Possible tableaux are: family portrait, tug-of-war, boredom, it's raining, on strike, a football lineup. Each dancer should memorize his starting position.

1. The group moves, elaborating on the situation suggested by the tableau, and finds an ending within one minute.

2. The group forms the same tableau. They take a moment to observe their shapes and placement relative to each other. They improvise, now using the tableau as a source of shapes, spatial relationships, and abstract movement ideas. They can find their own time limit, and come to an ending in stillness.

### CAPTIONS

This problem reverses the progression from literal to abstract. Now the dancers are asked to perceive literal interpretations of movement sequences.

**Procedure**  All the dancers begin off the space. A first person enters and begins to move. Others join in as they are ready and relate to the dancers in the space. They may leave and reenter as they wish. At any point someone

**Tableaux: Boredom**

may announce a caption for what is going on at that moment or what has happened up to that point. Everyone freezes, to end the improvisation. The dancers exit.

Someone enters to begin a new improvisation, which will end with a new caption. Repeat a number of times.

**Variations**  If the dancers get bogged down, without being able to find a caption, someone can time the improvisations, limiting them to one minute in length, calling out the time every fifteen seconds. Sometimes no caption will occur to anyone. The group should just go on to a new improvisation. They may pick up where they left off, if that seems promising. If there are few enough dancers that they can all see each other easily, they may stay in the space to begin again.

**Observations**  It is common for audience members to perceive story lines and images in even the most abstractly conceived dances. Here is a chance to find out what someone else sees in a situation. A caption may also be a purposefully funny interpretation of what is happening.

**WORD DUETS**

**Procedure**    One dancer enters and moves in the space, accompanying herself with a word or short word phrase. She may repeat the phrase or parts of the phrase as often as she chooses. Soon another dancer enters with his own word or word phrase, making a duet with the first dancer.

The dancers should focus on developing one aspect of their movement and sound relationship, rather than exploring all the possibilities. When some aspect of their relationship has been sufficiently developed, the first dancer leaves.

The second dancer continues moving, keeping his word phrase. Another dancer enters with her own phrase, in response to that of the second dancer. They create a duet in movement and sound.

The first time through, the series of duets should emphasize a literal interpretation of the words. In this case, the words can have dramatic connotations, as in the series, "Hold me!" "I'm leaving," "Someone's at the door," "Let me in!" The second time, it should focus on design, rhythm, and dynamics. In this case, it is best if the words have some connotations that can suggest movement motifs, as in the series, "Where are you going?" "Down and out," "Up, up and away!" and "Drop it!"

**Variations**    1. Three or more dancers can be in the space if people add on before anyone leaves. Dancers leave only when they feel that their leaving will help the improvisation more than their staying.

2. Without deciding whether to perform abstractly or dramatically, the dancers can let the level of abstraction change as new phrases enter the improvisation. They can let abstract and dramatic considerations coexist some of the time.

**Observation**    Dancers may also wear bits of costume to help them in their characterizations.

## MOOD AND CHARACTER

"His heart was hard against them." "It is a pressing issue." "He has a weak character."

In their everyday vocabulary people use many words, such as "hard," "pressing," and "weak," to describe moods and characters as well as movements. These verbal ambivalences reflect the fact that who we are and how we feel are revealed in our bodies and movement.

Some contemporary forms of psychotherapy are based on the mind-body connection and try to change the emotions by changing the body. In the arts, performers learn to embody their characters physically and to use movement as a vehicle of expression.

### DUETS: MOOD VARIATIONS

**Procedures**    The dancers are paired off. Each dancer is facing his partner.

1. One dancer in each pair chooses a mood or state of mind (which may or may not specifically be addressed to his partner), such as anger, fear, confusion, giddiness, and moves accordingly. The partner mirrors the movement as precisely as possible, including the mood. Dancers reverse roles and repeat, with a new mood.

2. Every dancer chooses a mood. One dancer in each pair is the leader, moving in accordance with his chosen mood. The partner mirrors the movement as much as possible except that she moves in accordance with her own chosen mood. Lamblike docility will have to soften the shapes, rhythm, and dynamics of leonine ferocity. The dancers should note what they must change in their movement to adapt to the difference in mood. Dancers reverse roles and repeat.

3. Each leader chooses a mood. The partner reacts to the leader's mood, with the freedom to do any movement and have any mood. Dancers reverse roles and repeat.

The first three procedures may be brief. Dancers may change partners between procedures.

4. Each leader chooses a mood. As in procedure 3, the partner reacts to the leader's mood, with the freedom to do any movement and have any mood. At any moment, however, the leader may choose to become the follower. When a dancer changes to the role of follower, she tries to do two things: react to her partner's mood and motivate the transition from her own mood to her reaction. One possible sequence would be anger, cowering, comforting, rejection, anger. Each pair should sense when it has reached a resolution and should end there.

**Observation**    The dancers should try to find physical embodiments of their moods and not rely on mugging.

## MOOD AND CHARACTER I

**Preparation** The leader teaches the whole group a phrase of movement that includes traveling and designed movement. A more advanced group can construct its own phrase.

**Procedure** The dancers divide into two groups which face each other in the space. The groups will take turns dancing.

Someone in one of the groups suggests a way to interpret the phrase, for example: militarily, romantically, drably, nervously, efficiently, brusquely, cordially, timidly. Working individually, all the dancers in the other group then interpret the phrase in this way. The groups alternate roles and repeat this procedure several times.

**Observation** The dancers may comment on the dynamics, rhythm, focus, or other movement characteristics that were basic to the various interpretations.

## MOOD AND CHARACTER II

**Procedures**  1. Each dancer makes a short phrase that creates a mood or character. One at a time they show their phrases.

2. The dancers interact in duets and trios, with each dancer adhering to his original motivation and using only his own phrase. Dancers may change the order of the movements and repeat parts of the phrase as they wish. This can be done all together or one group at a time, with the others watching.

3. The dancers arrange themselves into two groups, facing each other. Someone from one group names a mood or character. Everyone in the other group then moves, each one performing his own phrase in the mood or character named.

This procedure alternates between the two groups several times.

4. A group of five to eight dancers is in the space. Each dancer uses only his own movement phrase to interact with the others, but may allow the motivation to change in response to them.

**Observations** Some movement phrases might be more adaptable to certain moods or characters than to others. The dancers may be able to identify why this is so. For example, inward curving shapes may seem more serious or sad than open shapes. Focus, energy, or rhythm can also define the expressive quality of a movement. Do one or two of these aspects of movement determine the expression more than the others? Do different phrases depend on one element in particular for its expressive quality?

## MASKING THE FACE

**Preparation**    Using brown paper grocery bags, the dancers make masks using paint, crayons, marker pens, or cutouts. They should try to give the masks expression. Eyeholes must be included.

There should be a few extra bags left blank, with only eyeholes.

**Procedures**    1. Each dancer chooses a mask without seeing which it is. Each one also chooses a mood, attitude, or character. Wearing the mask, one dancer at a time moves according to the mood, attitude, or character he has chosen, which most likely will not be the same as the expression of the mask.

Which is stronger for the audience: the expression of the mask or the expression of the body?

2. Dancers repeat this, with blank bags. Does the movement still succeed in being expressive?

**Observations**    This problem may be more revealing for the dancers who are watching than for the dancers who are moving. If dancers can not rely on their faces for their expression, does their movement still transmit expression? Ideally the movement can speak for itself. The audience may even see more expression in the body when not distracted by the face.

## THE FACE

**Procedures**    Dancers join into pairs, facing each other for mirroring.

1. One of the dancers in each pair leads, moving her face only. She may explore both the physical range of movement of her face and the range of expression. The changes should be made slowly, so that the partner can mirror.

Dancers change roles and repeat.

2. The partners have a dialogue of facial expressions, taking turns. They may sometimes imitate their partner's expression but make it more or less intense, causing a gradual increase or reduction of expression. They may also react with a new attitude each turn.

The Face

3. Dancers keep the dialogue going and add body positions each turn. The body should support the expression in the face.

## YES NO WHY BECAUSE

Gretchen Russell, a student of mine, devised this improvisation for the class.

**Preparation**   For a group of four to eight dancers, each dancer chooses one of the four words: yes, no, why, because. All four words should be included in the choices. Each dancer also chooses one of these three moods: sad, angry, ecstatic.

**Procedure**   The dancers begin in the space. One dancer begins to move. The others gradually join in. Each dancer should move in accordance with the mood he has chosen and may say his word whenever he wants to. The way he says his word should also reflect his chosen mood. The dancers play off each other's moods and words.

A dancer may not change his word, but he may choose to change his mood. This shouldn't be done too often or arbitrarily.

Stillness is allowed.

**Observations**   If the dancers relax and play with this it can give wonderfully wacky results, especially because of the disjunction of the literal meanings of the words and the expression they are given here.

An ecstatic "no" can resound with happiness, and a sad "yes" echo with gloom.

The dancers should be aware of the patterns of silence and sound that they create, as well as the dramatic interactions.

### CONVERSATIONS

**Procedure**  All the dancers are in the space in still positions. At any time a dancer may walk through the space, approach a still figure, and make a "statement" of one or two movement phrases, ending in stillness. The person addressed responds with a short statement, ending in stillness. The conversation may end there; there may be further exchanges; or both may speak at once, as in real life.

The exchanges need not aim to mean anything. It is more the conversational encounter that is being explored.

A conversation may end either with both dancers in stillness, with one leaving, or with both leaving. A dancer may walk away to a new place and be still, or may approach another still figure for a conversation. A still figure wanting to initiate a conversation may approach someone.

There should always be pockets of stillness and sauntering during the piece.

**Observations**  Just as at a cocktail party, some conversations will take on momentum and continue for a while. Others will be concluded or abandoned after a brief exchange.

### RELATIONSHIPS

**Procedure**  Small groups of two to five dancers take turns in the space doing improvisations based on two related but contrasting instructions. Examples are strong and weak, meeting and parting, warmth and indifference, anger and appeasement, curiosity and boredom.

**Variation**  A group decides on a contrasting pair of instructions, without divulging what it is. The audience can guess.

### COMIC AND DRAMATIC ENTRANCES AND EXITS

**Procedure**  If possible, this should be done on a stage or in a space with flats at the sides to conceal dancers who have exited.

Dancers enter and exit when they wish, move across the space or return to the same side to exit. They should not linger in the space, but should spend whatever time it takes to make a "statement" with each entrance. This may be done by adding something to a motif that has already been introduced, reacting to something, commenting (in movement) on something, or introducing something new. There will sometimes be several dancers in the space at a time, sometimes only one or even none.

Dancers should pay special attention to their timing, considering comic or dramatic effect.

Offstage, two or more dancers may silently agree to enter together.

**Observations**     By performing their movement fully, using focus, speed, stillness, and design, the dancers should not need to mime their intentions. They should also be able to sense an appropriate ending.

This problem is usually funny and a good way to end a session.

## TYPES OF FOCUS

Improvisational work is based on the focus of attention to a given problem. It is also based on visual focus, since the interaction between the dancers depends on their seeing each other. In this sense there is a functional use of focus, which contact improvisors describe as "unfocused but perceiving."

In our human interactions we perceive other people's focus as an indication of their state of mind: attentive interest, glazed boredom, piercing intensity, wandering distraction, and so forth. Our emotional response to someone's focus is not very different when we watch them perform. A dancer's focus can reflect or motivate movement. In a formal way, it can clarify the direction of her movement and attention. In the expressive realm, reluctance or nostalgia turns away from the gesture; self absorption focuses inward; generosity includes the audience. The focus is an important theatrical tool for creating characterizations and expressing feelings.

### TYPES OF FOCUS

**Preparation**     The dancers name all the different types of focus they can think of. Examples include wandering, piercing, distant, fixed, inward, evasive, flickering, and darting.

**Procedures**     1. The group chooses one type of focus. All the dancers then improvise, motivating their movement with this focus. For example, they use evasive movement with an evasive focus.

If it is appropriate, dancers may relate to each other.

2. The group chooses one type of focus. All the dancers then improvise, contrasting their movement with the focus. For example, they use strong, direct movement with a wandering focus.

**Observations**   Some focuses, like flickering and darting, are almost immediately exhausting, and can be used only briefly. Any gaze, like a slow wandering or a steady, fixed stare, that allows for use of peripheral vision is related to the one dancers often use in improvisation.

Many of these focuses suggest psychological states, to which the dancers will have personal reactions.

### FOCUS DUETS

**Preparation**   Dancers pair off. Half the pairs are in the space, and half are audience. Each dancer silently chooses one type of focus.

**Procedure**   While maintaining his chosen focus, each dancer moves in relation to his partner. A dancer's movement may sometimes be motivated by his focus and sometimes be in contrast to it. Using the limitations of the chosen types of focus, the dancers should find ways to create duets.

**Observations**   Were certain focuses chosen more often than others? Why? What results from the various combinations of focus? Are some combinations more effective than others? For example, the pairing of a wandering focus with a fixed focus gives a situation of relatedness with contrast, and can be quite strong as a duet.

### FOCUS EVENTS

**Preparation**   The audience is at one end of the space. A group of three or four who will dance begins off the space.

**Procedure**   One at a time the dancers from the small group enter and move in the space, using their focus to motivate movement. Dancers may change their focus at any time.

The dancers should relate to each other as a group, trying to create some specific interaction among themselves.

When some event of interest has been created, the dancers find a way to exit.

This problem should be kept short, directed toward creating one specific interaction.

**Variation**   Dancers may plan the form of their event rather than discover it through improvisation. It should include a beginning, middle, and end.

**Observations**   The use of focus may be suggestive spatially, dramatically, and dynamically. Any of these realms may be used by the dancers to formulate their event. If necessary, the leader can suggest one means or another. Or do all three seem to be developed in each improvisation?

# BODY PARTS

All dancers have their own movement limitations, which may be determined by personality or body type, by lack of experience, by lack of training, or by entrenchment in prior training. A direct way to explore new movement possibilities is the isolation of parts of the body, moving them separately or as the motivation for movement of the whole body. Shy dancers get to move their faces and torsos. Unrestrained dancers can take this opportunity to be still and articulate fingers and toes.

## INDIVIDUAL BODY PARTS

**Procedures**   The dancers are distributed throughout the space.

1. The leader names one part of the body at a time: head, hands, arms, torso, right leg, both legs, eyes, mouth, face, shoulders, ribs, hips, elbows, knees, feet. Each dancer individually explores movement in each body part as it is named. Dancers should try to be specific in their movements: in shape, rhythm, and dynamics.

The leader may suggest types of movement: slow, fast, changing speeds, smooth, jerky, vibratory, low, high.

2. Each dancer individually explores ways one body part can initiate movement in the whole body. The dancers can explore stationary movement, traveling, turning, and change of level.

This may be done either by using one body part to move in various ways or by choosing a mode of movement and exploring the use of various body parts to motivate the movement. More advanced dancers may pay attention to the continuity and phrasing of their movements.

**Observation**   This problem can introduce dancers to movements beyond their habitual ranges.

### ONE BODY PART: ABA FORM

**Procedures**   1. The dancers are in the space. The leader names one body part.

One dancer begins to move, using the given body part to motivate his movement. Others gradually join in, using the same body part. Dancers may move the body part or use it to initiate full body movements, turns, travel, and changes of level.

The dancers should relate to each other, being aware of the group design, rhythms, and dynamics. To maintain coherence, dancers should imitate and vary each other's movements. Stillness is allowed and will help the pacing and coherence.

2. The leader names two body parts, A and B. The dancers structure their improvisation in an ABA form, changing their movement motivation from A to B and again later to A by silent group consensus. In the second A section they should repeat some of the movement used in the first section, and find an ending as a group.

**Observation**   Motivating movement with small body parts, like the wrists, may be more successful in this context than using larger, more central body parts, like the hips, because it allows the dancers to explore variety while keeping control. Sometimes moving central areas causes such large body changes that the dancers cannot define or control their movement choices as well.

### CONTINUOUS CONTACT

**Preparation**   Between one-half and two-thirds of the dancers join into pairs. The rest are solo figures. The pairs are in the space. Each pair has a point of physical contact between the two dancers, such as head to head or foot to thigh. The other dancers then distribute themselves in the space with attention to creating some group design.

**Procedure** The pairs begin to move, with the partners always remaining in contact with each other. The point of contact may remain the same or may change. The solo figures move freely, relating to the other solo figures or to the duets. The solos, having the greatest freedom, are responsible for forming the spatial composition of the entire group. They may also help coherence by imitating and varying movement occurring in the duets.

At any time, a solo figure may contact one member of a duet. At this point the other member of the duet must separate off, becoming a solo figure, leaving the other two to create a new duet.

To avoid being mistaken for a duet, solo figures may not touch each other. Dancers may be still at any time.

**Observations** Some duets are exciting because they explore a range of movement possibilities while keeping the same point of contact throughout. Other duets explore the perils of frequent changes of the points of contact.

# DYNAMICS

The dynamic is the force or energy of a movement, the attack and follow-through. With the rhythm, it forms the phrasing of sequences of movement. Dynamics can also be the vehicle for expressing emotions in dance. A body that is tense and strikes out conveys a different feeling from one that glides smoothly. Used both abstractly and mimetically, the dynamics of dance transform movement from a series of exercises into an art.

## SUSTAINED MOVEMENT AND ACCENTS

**Procedures** 1. All the dancers are in the space, moving continuously with no accents in their movement. They may speed up, slow down, or be still, and should avoid any accent when they start to move again after a stillness.

Dancers should try this first without any force in their movement, then with a muscular force or resistance.

2. All the dancers are in the space. They move continuously, occasionally adding accents and sudden stops. These may be forceful or light. Transitions between the smooth and accented movement should be clear and distinct. Dancers may sometimes come together into small groups and relate their accents together.

3. The dancers may now include movements that have dynamic elements other than sustained and accented: explosions of movement, jiggling, collapsing, shaking, bouncing. They should still try for clarity of transition from one dynamic to the next.

**Observations** Music can be added as a complement to this problem, either in support of the dynamics of the movement or in contrast.

Some dancers may begin to notice preferences in themselves for some dynamics over others. They can try the problem again, substituting new dynamics for their habitual range of movement.

### EXPLORING DYNAMICS

**Procedures** 1. The dancers divide into groups of three. One dancer in each group will be the leader, with the other two following. The leader will explore as full a range of dynamic variation as she can (light, heavy, stiff, jagged, sinuous, etc.). The followers imitate as closely as possible, aiming to reproduce the dynamic quality rather than the precise shape of the movement. The followers will sometimes have to fall behind in time. This is all right.

After a few minutes the dancers should be cued to stop. Then each group discusses the range of dynamics used by its leader, noticing if any dominated and if any were left out altogether.

Repeat two more times, rotating the leadership.

2. Once everyone has had a chance to lead, the groups make assignments for each of their members. For example, someone who tended to be light should move with weight; someone who was persistently sharp should be smooth.

One dancer from each group enters the space and moves in accordance with his assignment. The remaining two from each group observe. They may have further recommendations to offer. Each dancer gets a turn to move and get comments.

**Observations** The followers may also notice that they enjoy imitating certain dynamics more than others.

This problem, which gives the dancers a chance to observe their movement habits, can well be repeated periodically.

## FOUR AREAS

**Procedure**    The floor is divided into four areas of approximately equal size with clear dividing lines, as in figure 5.

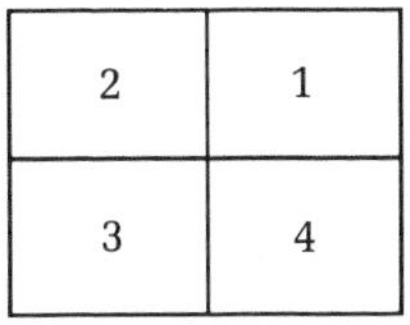

**Figure 5**

Each area has its own characteristic. One is a block of cold margarine through which the dancers have to carve their way. Two is visited by sudden, very strong gusts of wind. In three, gravity is four times as great as normal. In four, crawling, flying, and biting insects abound.

Dancers move in each area and go from one area to another. Transitions should be clear, whether they happen with a quick or gradual entry into the new area.

Half of the dancers may watch while half move.

**Variation**    Different images may be substituted for the ones given here.

## TWO CONTRASTING DYNAMICS

**Procedure**    A group of about five dancers is in the space. They choose two contrasting dynamics and improvise together, limited to moving within these two dynamics. The dancers may want to choose from this list: shaky, smooth, darting, heavy, forceful, abrupt, flickering, vibratory, floating, explosive, sharp, flitting, pressing, undulating. They can also come up with many other possibilities. The dancers should carry on no more than two movement motifs at one time and should keep the space well defined.

**Observations**    After each group has had a turn, the dancers may discuss which combinations of dynamics worked best for the performers and for the audience. Each group may then decide on a new pair of dynamics and repeat the procedure.

### DYNAMIC VARIATIONS

**Preparation**    The dancers join into two or more groups, with three to eight in each group. Each group makes up a phrase consisting of four or five different movements. Less advanced dancers may use these instructions to make their phrase: stretch, stamp, turn, lunge, and walk. More advanced dancers may not need instructions.

Each group should set its phrase so as to be able to perform it in near unison.

**Procedure**    One group at a time is in the space, improvising variations on its theme. In particular, the dancers should explore dynamic variations. To have some freedom, they may also vary the speed, direction, and order of movements in the phrase, and they may repeat parts of the phrase.

This improvisation shouldn't be directed at finding the widest range of possibilities, but at creating a strong interaction among the dancers.

## THEME AND VARIATIONS

The most common way to generate new movement is by creating a small amount of material and varying it in many ways. Some variations change the effect of the movement so that the source is not immediately recognizable; sometimes the variation is a more subtle change in the emphasis of the movement. The process of variation has the advantage of maintaining a relationship between the original material and the new material, which contributes to the coherence of the improvisation or work as a whole.

The work that follows uses both methodical and intuitive approaches for varying movement.

### WALKING VARIATIONS

**Procedure**    The dancers do a walking dance. They begin off the space and may enter and exit when they wish. They may use any variations on walking, discovering their options as they move. There should be no more than two events in the space at a time.

This may be accompanied by music.

**Observations**    The interest in this problem may arise out of formal results, in the dancers' use of the space, levels, rhythm, and dynamics, or out of characterizations emerging from the variations.

After identifying the variations used and discussing their consequences, the dancers may try the problem again.

## MIRRORING WITH VARIATIONS

**Procedures**    The dancers divide into pairs, for mirroring.

1. One dancer leads, not necessarily in such a way that the partner is able to mirror exactly. The partner sometimes mirrors exactly, and sometimes does variations on the leader's movement.

The dancers change roles and repeat.

The dancers may then observe which variations they used and which they tended to leave out. This list can be used as a reference.

| | |
|---|---|
| size | direction of travel |
| speed | level |
| rhythm | repetition |
| dynamics | change of order of movements |
| direction relative to the body | part of body |
| facing in the space | adding embellishments |
| travel | omitting part of the movement |

2. The pairs allow the leadership to pass back and forth between them. They should try to use some of the variations they haven't already used. A dancer can be frustrated in her attempt to vary movement if the person she is following keeps doing variations on her variations. For this reason, dancers should usually try to be aware of who is following and who is leading.

**Observations**    It is best if the leaders repeat some of their movement or establish some predictable patterns in their movement, to allow the followers time to respond.

The group leader can remind dancers to include any variations they tend to omit. Traveling and fast movement can transform a static duet into a more physically energetic one.

## WALKS AND VARIATIONS

**Procedure**    The whole group participates, and may enter and exit as they wish.

Combining their work in Walking Variations and Mirroring with Variations, the dancers improvise, using both walking motifs and other movement motifs. The dancers may use unison and canon as well as variations, and should be clear in their organization of the space. There should be no more than two events in the space at any time.

### VARIATIONS IN A CIRCLE

**Procedures**    1.  The dancers stand in a circle. One dancer begins by doing a single movement or a two-movement phrase, and repeats it continuously. As soon as they can, all the other dancers join in, moving in unison. They should try not to fall into mirroring instead of unison.

As soon as everyone is doing the movement, the initiator of that movement catches the eye of another dancer, who does a variation on the current movement. All the dancers, without stopping, make a transition to the new movement and repeat that.

This continues, with each new movement a variation on the last variation.

2.  Once every dancer has had a turn at making a variation, the whole group can try to reproduce the sequence of movements just created, identifying the variations used. This may help them to be aware of ones that have been used several times and the ones that have not been tried.

3.  Repeat the procedure, with dancers identifying aloud the variation they are using as they introduce their new phrases.

### COMBINING TWO SIMILAR PHRASES

**Preparation**    Each dancer makes a phrase based on a given set of instructions. One possible sequence is: jump, go down, get up, walk. Another is: twist, turn, run, shake. Each phrase should be repeatable.

**Procedure**    The group divides into trios. One or more of the trios is in the space at one time. In each trio, two of the dancers will do only their own phrases, varying the timing in order to relate their phrases to each other's. The similarity in original instructions should facilitate the relationship between the phrases.

The third dancer picks up movement from the other two, working to make good transitions between the two phrases, and to relate to the other two dancers. This dancer may also simultaneously do parts of both of the others' phrases, for example, the body design of one's jump with the steps of the other's walk.

This should be repeated so that each dancer gets a chance to be the combiner.

**Observations**    When dancers become excited by the interactions among themselves they can lose sight of the movement in favor of the relationships explored. Typically this takes the form of a great profusion of movement, an any-thing-will-serve approach. This exercise helps to refocus the dancers on their own movement and the movement of the others dancing with them.

### THREE ACTIONS

**Procedure**    The leader chooses three contrasting movements, such as tilt, turn, and run. All the dancers begin off the space. They may enter and exit as they wish. When in the space they must limit themselves to variations of the three given types of movement. The material should be used to make a well-composed group improvisation, considering use of space, and not allowing too much to be going on at any time.

The dancers repeat the procedure using other combinations of movements.

**Observations**    The dancers can note whether some combinations have better results.

Beginning choreographers sometimes have trouble setting limitations on the movement to include in their dances. This problem shows how much can be done with a limited repertory of movement.

### MAKING A THEMATIC PHRASE

In this case a thematic phrase is not a phrase with a theme, but a phrase that will be used as the basis for variations. Typically the phrase should be a chain of different movements, rather than the development of a motif.

**Procedures**    *Option 1.* The leader may give the dancers instructions, such as: travel, stretch, swing, stamp. Each dancer then makes his own phrase to these instructions, avoiding repetition, and combining the movement so that it is a dance phrase, and not a disjointed sequence of movement.

*Option 2.* With a more advanced group, instructions may not be necessary. Each dancer makes a phrase of three or four elements, avoiding repetition.

The dancers should show each other their phrases.

### EXPLORING VARIATIONS ON A THEME

Procedure    The dancers should choose one of the phrases made in the last problem, Making a Thematic Phrase, and all learn it. They may want to choose a phrase that has some variety in its design and energy.

The dancers work individually, trying out as many variations on the theme as they can. If needed, the leader may call out variations to remind the dancers of their options.

### GROUP VARIATIONS ON A THEME

Procedure    Half the group is in the space; half is audience. The group in the space improvises variations on the thematic phrase explored in the last problem. The dancers may move in unison with others, move in canon, initiate variations, or be still.

The group should limit itself to no more than two events in the space at a time.

### VARIATIONS ON IMPROVISED THEMES

Procedure    The dancers begin off the space. One dancer enters and presents a first thematic motif. Other dancers join in with variations on the theme, unison, canon, or stillness. At any time a second theme may be introduced, to be developed by the group. When either of these themes disappears, a new theme may be introduced. No more than two themes should be in the space at any time. An earlier theme may be reintroduced at a later time.

The dancers have a great deal of freedom in this problem and should try to integrate thematic variations with considerations of groupings, spacing, rhythm, and dynamics.

## PROPS

Props are so inspiring that dancers often respond instantly to them. There are many ways a prop can elicit movement. Dancers can pick them up and move them literally: sweeping the floor with a broom; or in a stylized or distorted way: sweeping the air or other dancers, enlarging or diminishing the gesture. They can imitate the movement made by the prop: bounce and roll like a ball, undulate like a scarf. Or they might discover a character by putting on a hat or a cloak, or picking up a cane. The dancers can move in and around the prop physically: sitting or standing or leaning on a chair. They can imitate with their movement the physical characteristics of the object: the jutting bristles of a brush, the smooth contours of a bar of soap, the repetitive regularity of the teeth of a comb.

All of these means will be tried out in the following problems, starting with setting a scene and letting the dancers loose in it.

## CHAIRS

**Procedure**    The leader places several chairs in the space. The dancers start by sitting, standing, and walking, and then may go on to explore the chairs however they can.

**Chairs**

Observations    The dancers may stand on the chairs, lean on them, move them to new locations, turn them upside down, crawl under them, carry them around. They may sit on someone's lap, take a chair out from under someone, share a chair with someone, sit on imaginary chairs, sit on the floor, or create tableaux.

Variations    Other props that can be used in similar ways are poles, cartons, pillows, rope, towels, umbrellas, and rolls of bathroom tissue. These are all big enough for the body to relate to in design, and all small enough to move and carry.

## PAPER BAGS

Preparation    Dancers bring in large, paper grocery bags, about two per person.

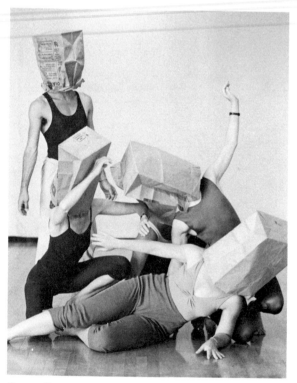

**Paper Bags**

**Procedures**    1. Half the dancers watch. The other half put paper bags over their heads, so that they can't see. They begin around the edge of the space. They work their way into the center, sending signals by making noise with their bags. The dancers gather in the center and try to create a dance only by feel and by sound. Then they disperse to the edges of the space and end.

Dancers reverse roles and repeat.

2. The dancers are given a simple floor pattern to follow, such as going diagonally across the space. Half the dancers watch and half travel across the space with bags on their heads. Even though they can't see each other, the dancers should try to interact as a group. Note that, despite their best intentions, the dancers may not be able to accomplish the floor pattern.

This can sharpen a dancer's awareness of others. This situation provides the protection and the challenge of performing for an audience without having one's face visible. (See also Masking the Face in the section on Mood and Character.)

3. The whole group is in the space, each with his own bag or two. The bags can be used in any way, always with the idea of interacting with other dancers.

Dancers may tear the bags so as to wear them on other parts of their body, stuff their leotards, skate on the paper . . .

## BALLS

**Preparation**    The leader or group brings in a collection of balls, large and small. Dancers individually explore movement by relating to the balls in several ways. They may move the balls, roll and bounce them, and, if there are no windows or mirrors to break, throw and kick them. They may repeat and stylize these movements without the balls. They may roll and bounce like balls. They may imitate the round shape of balls.

**Procedure**    A group of dancers begins in the space, in a still design, with a number of balls. Others are off the space. Dancers may enter and exit at any time.

The dancers use the balls to find ways to move and to interact among themselves. They should allow only two events to occur in the space at a time.

## PROP DUETS

**Preparation**    The leader or group brings in a variety of props that can be handled or moved by a single dancer, preferably something that is pliant and can change shape: fabric, a dust mop, paper bags, a magazine, a sponge, a rubber band, a backpack, a rope.

**Procedure**    Two dancers are in the space. One has a prop, which she will move in various ways. The other dancer performs a duet with the prop by imitating or varying the prop's movement using all or parts of his body.

The dancer who is handling the prop should try to move it in such a way that she helps the other dancer. This may include repeating movements and playing with the size and speed of the movements. She should also respond to what the dancer is doing, change if the dancer seems stuck for a long time and stay with one type of movement if it is going well. She should also be aware of her own movement as she handles the prop, and should be part of the performance.

All dancers should get a turn at each role.

**Observation**    Some props work better than others. Why?

## EXPLORING PROPS

**Preparation**    The leader and dancers bring in props, at least one for each person. There may be duplicates.

**Procedures**    1. All the dancers are in the space. Dancers work individually, each one having a prop to use as a source of movement. A dancer might explore the round, smooth, heaviness of a rock, or the floating of a feather, or the repetitive rhythm suggested by the teeth of a comb, or the flatness of a piece of paper. A dancer might move the prop, then repeat the same movements without the prop. Each prop will suggest a different method of exploration, as well as different movements.

When a dancer has finished with a prop, he puts it into a common pool of props and takes another. Each dancer should explore all the props.

2. The group decides on two props that were most inspiring and that can provide some contrast in movement. Without using any props, only recalling the feel, weight, movement, and shape of the props, the danc-

ers make a group improvisation based on the two chosen props. They should avoid mime.

This can be done with half the group at a time. If the other half doesn't know which props were chosen they might try to guess, based on the shapes, dynamics, and rhythms that they see in the movement of the other group.

**Observations**   Why do some props work better than others? Why do some combinations work better than others?

### USING THE ENVIRONMENT

**Procedure**   The dancers or the leader chooses an environment. This could be a staircase, a grove of trees, a playground, a telephone booth, a picnic table, a bus stop, a doorway, a squash court. Using the shapes and relationships suggested by the location, the dancers respond to the environment and improvise together. They should not allow the environment to totally distract them from relating to each other.

**Observation**   The dancers may find that they need to suggest limitations in order to help them work together as a group.

## SOUND ACCOMPANIMENT

Each person may be looking in a different direction at any time and seeing different things. But everyone will hear the same sounds at the same time. Therefore, sound has the power to unify a group.

Music in particular has a strong power to suggest movement styles, rhythm, and energy. If the dancers learn to listen and react attentively, they can learn to play with and against the music or other sound so that the accompaniment enhances the movement rather than dominating it.

The dancers can also learn to add a dimension to their improvisations by creating the sound accompaniment themselves.

### DANCING TO MUSIC

**Preparation**   The leader or dancers bring in a wide range of recorded music: baroque, classical, romantic, contemporary, popular, rock, folk music of America and other cultures, soul, jazz.

**Procedure** Entering and exiting when they wish, the dancers move in response to the music, also relating to one another, so that there are no more than two events at a time.

**Observations** The dancers may begin by responding to the most obvious aspects of the music: the style if a movement style is associated with the music, or the meter and dynamics. They may eventually respond to the instrumentation: the difference between a melody played on an oboe and on a piano, to the pitch, to the breath and phrasing of the music. Different pieces of music will suggest different areas of response.

### MIRRORING WITH MUSIC

**Procedures** The dancers divide into pairs. Music is played.

1. One member of each pair moves in response to the music. As with all mirroring, the leader has to keep her eyes on her partner and may not move through the mirror. The partner mirrors as best he can.

2. Still mirroring, the leadership passes back and forth between partners.

3. The two partners may simultaneously explore contrasting or complementary movement in response to different aspects of the music. This may be the rhythm in different instruments, or different dynamic qualities. They may sometimes choose to mirror.

### DANCING WITH AND AGAINST MUSIC

**Procedure** An "east-west" axis is established in the space, which divides the "north" from the "south" (see fig. 6).

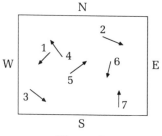

**Figure 6**

Irrespective of where a dancer is located in the space, if he's facing anywhere in the 180 degree range to the north, he moves with the music. When a dancer is facing anywhere in the 180 degree range to the south, he moves against the music. In the figure, 4, 5, and 7 are facing north and 1, 2, 3, and 6 are facing south.

As a dancer turns and changes his facing in the space, he must change his relation to the music if he turns past the east-west axis.

In this way, dancers may travel anywhere in the space, moving with the music, or against it, as long as they don't turn past the axis. On the other hand, they may also play with the transitions by frequently changing direction.

This problem may be further defined by limiting one element at a time. Dancers would then move with or against the speed, rhythm, style, dynamic quality, or mood of the music.

**Observations**    Can the dancers find a variety of ways to go against the music? For example, to go against the rhythm they can be spasmodic, nonmetrical, sustained, syncopated, or move to a different pulse.

## SOUND PRODUCTION

**Procedure**    The dancers stand in a circle. One dancer begins by making some sound or pattern of sounds, and continues to repeat it. One dancer at a time adds a sound to those already happening. A dancer may choose to support, vary, or contrast someone else's sound. A dancer may stop his sound at any time. He may then introduce a new sound at any time. The dancers should choose their sound patterns and when to be quiet again in response to what is going on. Some sounds may be steady; others may be used as infrequent punctuations. The overall sound should not be so dense that it becomes muddy.

The dancers should use this time to explore the various ways they have to produce sound. For example, with their hands they may clap, snap, rub; with their mouths they may cluck, click, whistle, hiss; with their voices they may hum, hoot, groan, laugh, whine, yowl; with their feet they may stamp or shuffle.

## SOUND ACCOMPANIMENT

**Procedure**  A trio produces sound accompaniment, using some of the sounds explored in Sound Production. They should give some pattern to their sounds and relate them to each other. Accompaniment may be metrical or not.

A solo figure moves in the space in response to the sound. The audience may comment on the relationship between the sound and the movement.

**Variations**  1. This may also be done with two or three dancers relating to each other as well as to the sound.

2. Reversing the interaction, an individual or group of dancers moves and the sound responds to the movement.

3. The initiative passes back and forth between dancers and accompanists, in an unplanned way.

**Note**  See the problem on Rhythmic Accompaniment in the section on Metrical Rhythm, with single accompanists responding to individual dancers.

## CROSSINGS

**Procedure**  Dancers stand on opposite sides of the space or in the wings, if there are any. At any time a dancer may move across the space, accompanying his own movement with sound. Crossings may be fast or slow, alone or with someone, crowded or sparse. Sounds may be constant or occasional. Dancers should use imitation, repetition, variation, and contrast as means to relate to each other.

## VOICE PRACTICE

**Procedures**  The dancers stand in a circle.
1. *Range.*
   a. On a vowel sound everyone hits a high note and slides down his range to a low note. On each repeat, the dancers can aim to begin higher and end lower, until they feel they've covered the range of their voices. They should stand easily erect and keep their jaws and throats relaxed, repeating this exercise until the resonance of the voices is full.

The leader may direct the group to begin together, or they may begin sequentially, causing a cascade of pitches.

b. One dancer hits a note anywhere in her range, high, middle, or low, and sustains it. When the note dies away, the next dancer hits a note in a contrasting range. This continues around the circle.

c. One dancer hits a note and sustains it while all the others match the pitch. The next dancer then hits a note in a contrasting range, and everyone matches it. This continues around the circle.

The dancers should continue to relax their jaws and throats and to support the sound with their breath.

2. *Volume.* Proceeding around the circle, each dancer in turn says a sentence, varying the volume, including both loud and soft sounds. Dancers may want to relate their sentences to the preceding ones, either in the sense of the words or in the pattern of volume.

3. *Speed.* Proceeding around the circle, each dancer in turn says one word very slowly, followed by a sentence very quickly. On their second turns, the dancers may intersperse the slow and fast in their sentences.

4. *Range, volume, and speed.* Each dancer in turn says a few sentences, including some high, some low, some loud, some soft, some fast, and some slow sounds.

**Observations**    These exercises help warm up the voice. Giving the dancer specific goals in their sound production can lessen their self-consciousness; relating the words, range, volume, and speed to what has come before introduces a compositional awareness to the use of words. Dancers should be encouraged to explore the extreme ranges of sound production.

### NAMES AND NICKNAMES

**Procedures**    1. The dancers walk throughout the space, meeting the eyes of other dancers, saying their own names whenever they want to. The walk may vary in direction and speed.

2. When two dancers meet they say their own names or each other's names, adding movement. They continue moving together, creating a brief duet, then part and continue walking until they join someone else for a duet.

They should try to use the space fully, so that the duets don't become one mass in the center of the space.

3. The dancers stand in a circle. Considering one dancer at a time, they should come up with nicknames that sound like the dancer's name. The nicknames should be real words. For example, Joyce could give juice, joyous, or choice. Everyone should have a turn to get nicknames. The dancers then may walk, be still, or join into duets or small groups, saying names or nicknames and making brief group dances together. Without being mimed, the nicknames may suggest a mood or style of movement. Joyce (joyous) and Mary (merry) might have a celebratory duet. Heather (feather) might inspire floating, wispy, or even quill-sharp movement.

**Observations**    Although procedures 1 and 2 are good for letting a new group of dancers get familiar with each other, procedure 3 works only if the dancers already know each other's names and don't have to struggle to recall or make up nicknames.

### SOMETHING EXTREME

**Procedure**    One dancer at a time is in the space, with one instruction: to use both voice and movement and do something extreme. Dancers may have a few minutes first to consider a plan of action.

**Observations**    Beginning dancers in particular sometimes need encouragement to let loose and do more than they imagine is acceptable. Some people have to try to be extreme to see that they can go much further.

This is not the case for everyone. A student of mine who had strained her ankle sat on a chair and vehemently talked about what it was like to be injured, how badly people treated her, how left out she felt. Shouting and gesticulating in her genuine effort to get her point across, she leaned forward and fell out of her chair.

List of Improvisations

Bibliography

Index

# List of Improvisations

The columns indicate (A) whether an improvisation can be done as a solo, (B) what size group is recommended, and whether the improvisation requires (C) no prior experience or (D) some prior experience. Check marks in both skill levels mean that prior experience may not be necessary but may make a notable difference in the outcome of the improvisation, or that different parts of the improvisation are appropriate for different levels.

| Page | Improvisation | A | B | C | D |
|------|---------------|---|---|---|---|
| | **PRELIMINARIES** | | | | |
| 3 | Action Word Warmup | • | any | • | |
| 4 | Body Parts Warmup | • | any | • | |
| 4 | Locomotor Warmup | | any | • | |
| | **Mirroring** | | | | |
| 5 | Mirroring | | duets | • | |
| 6 | Mirroring with Succession | | duets | • | |
| 6 | Mirroring with Movement Variations | | duets | • | |
| 7 | Group Mirror | | 6–12 | • | |
| | **Unison** | | | | |
| 8 | Name Accumulation | | 3–16 | • | |
| 8 | Group Unison | | 3 + | • | |
| 10 | Following Two Leaders | | 5 + | • | |
| 10 | Three Unison Groups without Leaders | | 6 + | • | |
| | **Active and Passive** | | | | |
| 11 | Moving with Closed Eyes | | any | • | |
| 11 | Leading Someone with Closed Eyes | | duets | • | |
| 12 | Active/Passive Duets | | duets | • | |
| 13 | Active/Passive Group | | 5–20 | • | |
| | **Weight Dependency** | | | | |
| 13 | Weight Dependency for Two Dancers | | duets | • | |
| 15 | Falls and Catches | | trios | • | |
| 15 | Weight Dependency for a Group | | 3 + | • | |
| 16 | Duet Scenes | | duets | • | |

A: Suitable for Solo

B: Recommended Group Size

C: No Prior Experience Needed

D: Prior Experience Helpful

A: Suitable for Solo                    C: No Prior Experience Needed
B: Recommended Group Size        D: Prior Experience Helpful

| Page | Improvisation | A | B | C | D |
|---|---|---|---|---|---|
| | **Group Design** | | | | |
| 41 | Symmetrical and Asymmetrical Shapes | • | any | • | |
| 41 | Symmetrical Group Tableaux | | 6 + | • | |
| 43 | Addition and Subtraction | | 6 + | • | |
| | **Shape and Shape Sequences** | | | | |
| 45 | Individual Shapes | | any | • | |
| 45 | Hand Dialogues | | duets | • | |
| 47 | Quartets: Taking Shapes | | 4 + | • | |
| 48 | Waves of Movement | | 6 | • | |
| 49 | Shape Canon | | any | • | |
| 50 | Moving a Shape | • | 3–8 | • | |
| 51 | Moving a Series of Shapes | | 3–5 | | • |
| 52 | Moving a Shape: Duets | | duets | • | |
| | **Trace Designs** | | | | |
| 53 | Volumes I | • | any | • | |
| 54 | Volumes II | • | any | • | |
| 54 | Volumes III | • | any | • | |
| 54 | Individual Trace Designs | • | any | • | |
| 55 | Circles and Straight Lines | • | any | • | |
| 55 | Mock Orange | | any | • | |
| | **TIME** | | | | |
| | **Pulse** | | | | |
| 59 | Keeping a Steady Pulse: Clapping | | any | • | |
| 60 | Keeping a Steady Pulse: Traveling | | any | • | |
| 60 | Subdividing a Pulse | | any | • | |
| 61 | Locomotor Movements | | any | • | |
| 61 | Free Movement to a Pulse | | any | • | |
| | **Accent** | | | | |
| 62 | Accenting Random Beats | | any | • | |
| 62 | Measures of Two, Three, Four, and Five Beats | | any | • | |
| 63 | Clapping Meters I | | up to 15 | • | |
| 64 | Clapping Meters II: Mixed Meters | | up to 15 | • | |
| 64 | Accents in Counterpoint | | any | • | • |
| 66 | Mixed Meter: Counterpoint | | any | • | • |
| 67 | Omitted Beats | • | any | • | |
| 67 | Syncopation | • | any | • | |
| 68 | Individual Rhythmic Accents | • | any | • | |
| 68 | Eight-Count Rhythmic Phrases | | duets | • | |
| 68 | Group Rhythmic Accents | | 3–4 | • | |

A: Suitable for Solo                     C: No Prior Experience Needed
B: Recommended Group Size          D: Prior Experience Helpful

| Page | Improvisation | A | B | C | D |
|---|---|:---:|:---:|:---:|:---:|
| | **Metrical Rhythm** | | | | |
| 69 | Clapping Rhythms | | any | • | • |
| 70 | Reproducing Rhythms | | any | • | • |
| 70 | Walking Rhythms | | duets | • | • |
| 71 | Rhythmic Movement: Trios | | trios | • | • |
| 72 | Rhythmic Accompaniment | | any | • | • |
| 73 | Rhythmic Counterpoint: A Round | | any | | • |
| 74 | Canon | | 3–4 | | • |
| | **Nonmetrical Rhythms** | | | | |
| 75 | Counting Numbers | | any | • | |
| 75 | Nonmetric Phrase Sequences | | any | • | |
| 75 | Nonmetric Sound and Movement | • | any | • | |
| 76 | Single Movements | • | any | • | |
| 77 | Phrase Lengths | | 5–10 | • | |
| 77 | Breath Phrases | • | any | • | |
| 78 | Loose Canon | | trios | • | |
| 78 | Rhythmic Variations | | any | • | • |
| | **Duration and Speed** | | | | |
| 79 | Estimating Duration | • | any | • | |
| 80 | Repetition and Duration | | any | • | |
| 80 | 87654321 | • | 6–10 | • | |
| 81 | Fast, Medium, and Slow | | 3–8 | • | |
| 82 | Acceleration and Deceleration | | trios | • | |
| 82 | Sudden Changes of Speed | | any | • | |
| 83 | Contrasts | | 3–5 | • | |
| 83 | Variations on Speed | | 4–5 | • | • |
| | **MOVEMENT INVENTION** | | | | |
| | **Images** | | | | |
| 85 | Environments | • | any | • | |
| 86 | Quick Images | | any | • | |
| 86 | Animals | • | any | • | |
| 87 | Laugh, Giggle, Sob | • | any | • | |
| 88 | Simple Movement Vignettes | | 3–5 | • | |
| 88 | Narratives | • | up to 10 | • | |
| 89 | Clichés | • | up to 8 | • | |
| | **Levels of Abstraction** | | | | |
| 91 | Hand Gestures | | duets | • | |
| 92 | Dramatic Intentions | | 3–5 | • | |

A: Suitable for Solo  
B: Recommended Group Size  
C: No Prior Experience Needed  
D: Prior Experience Helpful

A: Suitable for Solo

B: Recommended Group Size

C: No Prior Experience Needed

D: Prior Experience Helpful

# Bibliography

## IMPROVISATION AND COMPOSITION

**DANCE**

Barlin, Anne Lief, and Greenberg, Tamar Robbin. *Move and be Moved: A Practical Approach to Movement with Meaning.* Los Angeles: Learning Through Movement, 1980.

Barry, Thais Grace. "Improvisation for Modern Dance: Implications for Dance Education." Ed. D. dissertation, Columbia Teachers College, 1977.

Bartal, Lea, and Ne'eman, Nira. *Movement Awareness and Creativity.* New York: Harper and Row, 1975.

Blom, Lynne Anne, and Chaplin, L. Tarin. *The Intimate Act of Choreography.* Pittsburgh: University of Pittsburgh Press, 1982.

Ellfeldt, Lois. *A Primer for Choreographers.* Palo Alto, Calif.: National Press Books, 1967.

Findlay, Elsa. *Rhythm and Movement: Applications of Dalcroze Eurythmics.* Evanston, Ill.: Summy-Birchard, 1971.

Hawkins, Alma. *Creating Through Dance.* Englewood Cliffs, N.J.: Prentice-Hall, 1964.

Hayes, Elizabeth R. *Dance Composition and Production.* New York: Dance Horizons, 1981.

H'Doubler, Margaret. *The Dance.* New York: Harcourt, Brace, 1925.

———. *Dance: A Creative Art Experience.* New York: F. S. Crofts, 1940.

Humphrey, Doris. *The Art of Making Dances.* New York: Rinehart, 1959.

Lockhart, Aileene S., and Pease, Esther E. *Modern Dance: Building and Teaching Lessons.* 6th ed. Dubuque, Iowa: Wm. C. Brown, 1982.

Mettler, Barbara. *Group Dance Improvisations.* Tucson: Mettler Studies, 1975.

———. *Materials of Dance as a Creative Art Activity.* Tucson: Mettler Studios, 1960.

Preston-Dunlop, Valerie. *A Handbook for Modern Educational Dance.* Boston: Plays, 1980.

Shafranski, Paulette. *Modern Dance: Twelve Creative Problem-Solving Experiments.* Glenview, Ill.: Scott, Foresman, 1985.

Smith, Jacqueline. *Dance Composition: A Practical Guide for Teachers.* Surrey: Lepus Books, 1976.

Turner, Margery J., with Grauert, Ruth, and Zallman, Arlene. *New Dance: Approaches to Nonliteral Choreography.* Pittsburgh: University of Pittsburgh Press, 1971.

**THEATER**

Benedetti, Robert L. *The Actor at Work.* 3rd ed. Englewood Cliffs, N.J.: Prentice-Hall, 1981.

Hodgson, John, and Richards, Ernest. *Improvisation.* New York: Grove Press, 1966.

King, Nancy. *Theatre Movement: The Actor and His Space.* New York: Drama Book Specialists, 1971.

Penrod, James. *Movement for the Performing Artist.* Palo Alto, Calif.: Mayfield, 1974.
Spolin, Viola. *Improvisation for the Theater: A Handbook of Teaching and Directing Techniques.* Evanston, Ill.: Northwestern University Press, 1963.

### DANCE THERAPY

Bernstein, Penny Lewis. *Theory and Methods in Dance-Movement Therapy: A Manual for Therapists, Students, and Educators.* Dubuque, Iowa: Kendall/Hunt Pub., 1972.

## OF INTEREST

### DANCE

*Ballet Review* 1, no. 6 (1967).
Banes, Sally. *Terpsichore in Sneakers: Post-Modern Dance.* Boston: Houghton Mifflin, 1980.
Copeland, Roger. "Merce Cunningham and the Politics of Perception." In *What Is Dance? Readings in Theory and Criticism.* Edited by Roger Copeland and Marshall Cohen. Oxford: Oxford University Press, 1983.
*Dance Scope* 14, no. 4 (1980).
Denby, Edwin. *Dancers, Buildings and People in the Streets.* New York: Popular Library, 1965.
Halprin, Ann. "Intuition and Improvisation in Dance." *Impulse* (1955): 10–12.
———. "The Process Is the Purpose: An Interview with Vera Maletic." *Dance Scope* 4 (1967/68): 11–18.
Horst, Louis, and Russell, Carroll. *Modern Dance Forms in Relation to the Other Modern Arts.* New York: Dance Horizons, 1967.
Laban, Rudolf von. *Choreutics.* London: Macdonald and Evans, 1966.
———. *The Mastery of Movement.* London: Macdonald and Evans, 1960.
Litvinoff, Valentina. *The Use of Stanislavsky Within the Modern Dance.* New York: American Dance Guild, 1972.
McDonagh, Donald. *The Rise and Fall and Rise of Modern Dance.* New York: New American Library, 1970.
Paxton, Steve. "Contact Improvisation." *The Drama Review* 19, no. 1 (1975): 40–42.
Rainer, Yvonne. "Yvonne Rainer Interviews Ann Halprin." *The Drama Review* 10, no. 2 (1965): 142–66.

### THEATER

Blumenthal, Eileen. *Joseph Chaikin: Exploring at the Boundaries of Theater.* Directors in Perspective. Cambridge: Cambridge University Press, 1984.
Croyden, Margaret. *Lunatics, Lovers and Poets: The Contemporary Experimental Theatre.* New York: McGraw-Hill, 1974.
Fleshman, Bob, ed. *Theatrical Movement: A Bibliographical Anthology.* Metuchen, N.J.: The Scarecrow Press, 1986.
Goldberg, RoseLee. *Performance: Live Art 1909 to the Present.* New York: Harry N. Abrams, 1979.
Henri, Adrian. *Total Art: Environments, Happenings, and Performance.* New York: Praeger, 1974.

Johnstone, Keith. *Impro: Improvisation and the Theatre.* London: Methuen, 1981.
Kirby, Michael. *The Art of Time: Essays on the Avant-garde.* New York: E. P. Dutton, 1969.
———. *Happenings: An Illustrated Anthology.* New York: Dutton, 1965.
———. "The New Theatre." *Tulane Drama Review* 10, no. 2 (winter 1965): 23–43.
———, ed. *The New Theatre: Performance Documentation.* New York: New York University Press, 1974.
Shank, Theodore. *American Alternative Theatre.* New York: Grove Press, 1982.
Sweet, Jeffrey. *Something Wonderful Right Away.* New York: Avon Books, 1978.

## THERAPY

Feder, Elaine, and Feder, Bernard. *The Expressive Arts Therapies.* Englewood Cliffs, N.J.: Prentice-Hall, 1981.
Fleshman, Bob, and Fryrear, Jerry L. *The Arts in Therapy.* Chicago: Nelson-Hall, 1981.
Lefco, Helene. *Dance Therapy: Narrative Case Histories of Therapy Sessions with Six Patients.* Chicago: Nelson-Hall, 1974.
Rosen, Elizabeth. *Dance in Psychotherapy.* Brooklyn, N.Y.: Dance Horizons, 1974.

## OTHER

Arnheim, Rudolf. *Visual Thinking.* Berkeley and Los Angeles: University of California Press, 1969.
Bailey, Derek. *Musical Improvisation: Its Nature and Practice in Music.* Englewood Cliffs, N.J.: Prentice-Hall, 1980.
Ghiselin, Brewster, ed. *The Creative Process: A Symposium.* New York: New American Library, 1952.

# Index

Entries in bold type are names of improvisations.